W9-BZP-759

Weekly Reader:
SUMMER EXPRESS

New York • Toronto • London • Auckland • Sydney
Mexico City • New Delhi • Hong Kong • Buenos Aires

Editor: Ourania Papacharalambous
Cover and interior design by Michelle H. Kim

ISBN: 978-1-338-10890-3
Compilation and illustrations copyright © 2017 by Scholastic Inc.
All rights reserved.
Printed in the U.S.A.
First printing, January 2017.

9 10 11 12   40   23 22 21 20

Table of Contents

Dear Parent,

Congratulations! You hold in your hands an exceptional educational tool that will give your child a head start in the coming school year.

Inside this book, you'll find 100 practice pages that will help your child review and learn reading and writing skills, grammar, place value, addition and subtraction, and so much more! *Weekly Reader: Summer Express* is divided into 10 weeks, with two practice pages for each day of the week, Monday through Friday. However, feel free to use the pages in any order that your child would like. Here are other features you'll find inside:

★ A weekly incentive chart and certificate to motivate and reward your child for his or her efforts.

★ Ideas for fun, skill-building activities you can do with your child any time.

★ Suggestions for creative learning activities that you can do with your child each week.

★ A certificate of completion to celebrate your child's accomplishments.

We hope you and your child will have a lot of fun as you work together to complete this workbook.

Enjoy!

The Editors

Tips for Using This Book

1. Pick a good time for your child to work on the activities. You may want to do it around mid-morning after play, or early afternoon when your child is not too tired.

2. Make sure your child has all the supplies he or she needs, such as pencils and an eraser. Designate a special place for your child to work.

3. Have stickers handy as rewards. Celebrate your child's accomplishments by letting him or her affix stickers to the incentive chart after completing the activities each day.

4. Encourage your child to complete the worksheets, but don't force the issue. While you may want to ensure that your child succeeds, it's also important that he or she maintains a positive and relaxed attitude toward school and learning.

5. After you've given your child a few minutes to look over the activity pages he or she will be working on, ask your child to tell you his or her plan of action: "Tell me about what we're doing on these pages." Hearing the explanation aloud can provide you with insights into your child's thinking processes. Can he or she complete the work independently? With guidance? If your child needs support, try offering a choice about which family member might help. Giving your child a choice can help boost confidence and help him or her feel more ownership of the work to be done.

6. When your child has finished the workbook, present him or her with the certificate of completion on page 143. Feel free to frame or laminate the certificate and display it on the wall for everyone to see. Your child will be so proud!

Skill-Building Activities for Any Time

The following activities are designed to complement the 10 weeks of practice pages in this book. These activities don't take more than a few minutes to complete and are just a handful of ways in which you can enrich and enliven your child's learning. Use the activities to take advantage of time you might ordinarily disregard—for example, standing in line at the supermarket. You'll be working to practice key skills and have fun together at the same time.

Find Real-Life Connections

One of the reasons for schooling is to help children function in the real world, to empower them with the abilities they'll truly need. So why not put those developing skills into action by enlisting your child's help with creating a grocery list, reading street signs, sorting pocket change, and so on? He or she can apply reading, writing, science, and math skills in important and practical ways, connecting what he or she is learning with everyday tasks.

An Eye for Patterns

A red-brick sidewalk, a beaded necklace, a Sunday newspaper—all show evidence of structure and organization. You can help your child recognize the way things are structured, or organized, by observing and talking about patterns they see. Your child will apply his or her developing ability to spot patterns across all school subject areas, including alphabet letter formation (writing), attributes of shapes and solids (geometry), and characteristics of narrative stories (reading). Being able to notice patterns is a skill shared by effective readers and writers, scientists, and mathematicians.

Journals as Learning Tools

Most of us associate journal writing with reading comprehension, but having your child keep a journal can help you keep up with his or her developing skills in other academic areas as well—from telling time to matching rhymes. To get started, provide your child with several sheets of paper, folded in half, and stapled together. Explain that he or she will be writing and/or drawing in the journal to complement the practice pages completed each week. Encourage your child to draw or write about what he or she found easy, what was difficult, or what was fun. Before moving on to another set of practice pages, take a few minutes to read and discuss that week's journal entries together.

Promote Reading at Home

- Let your child catch you in the act of reading for pleasure, whether you like reading science fiction novels or do-it-yourself magazines. Store them someplace that encourages you to read in front of your child and **demonstrate that reading is an activity you enjoy**. For example, locate your reading materials on the coffee table instead of your nightstand.

- Set aside a family reading time. By designating a reading time each week, your family is assured an opportunity to discuss with each other what you're reading. You can, for example, share a funny quote from an article. Or your child can tell you his or her favorite part of a story. The key is to **make a family tradition of reading and sharing books** of all kinds together.

- **Put together collections of reading materials** your child can access easily. Gather them in baskets or bins that you can place in the family room, the car, and your child's bedroom. You can refresh your child's library by borrowing materials from your community's library, buying used books, or swapping books and magazines with friends and neighbors.

Skills Alignment

Listed below are the skills covered in the activities throughout *Weekly Reader: Summer Express*. These skills will help children review what they know while helping prevent summer learning loss. They will also better prepare each child to meet, in the coming school year, the math and language arts learning standards established by educators.

Math

	Week 1	Week 2	Week 3	Week 4	Week 5	Week 6	Week 7	Week 8	Week 9	Week 10
Represent and solve problems involving addition and subtraction.	✦		✦	✦		✦	✦		✦	✦
Understand the relationship between addition and subtraction.			✦	✦		✦	✦	✦		
Add and subtract within 20.	✦	✦	✦	✦			✦	✦	✦	✦
Work with addition and subtraction equations.	✦		✦	✦			✦	✦	✦	✦
Extend the counting sequence.		✦	✦					✦	✦	
Understand place value.	✦	✦	✦	✦	✦	✦				✦
Use understanding of place value to add and subtract.				✦	✦		✦	✦	✦	✦
Measure lengths indirectly and by iterating length units.	✦		✦		✦	✦				
Tell and write time.		✦				✦			✦	✦
Represent and interpret data.			✦		✦				✦	
Reason with shapes and their attributes.	✦				✦			✦		✦

Language Arts

	Week 1	Week 2	Week 3	Week 4	Week 5	Week 6	Week 7	Week 8	Week 9	Week 10
Ask and answer questions about key details.	✦	✦	✦	✦	✦	✦	✦	✦	✦	✦
Identify the main topic or central message and retell key details.	✦	✦	✦	✦	✦	✦	✦	✦	✦	✦
Describe characters, settings, and major events in a story.	✦	✦	✦							✦
Describe connections in a text and explain differences among text types.		✦	✦							
Know and use text features.						✦				
Identify the narrator at various points in a story.	✦								✦	
Distinguish source of information within a text.										✦
Use images and details within a text to describe the text.					✦		✦	✦		
Identify an author's points in a text.										✦
Compare and contrast two texts.					✦			✦		
Demonstrate understanding of the organization and basic features of print.	✦	✦							✦	
Demonstrate understanding of spoken words, syllables, and sounds.		✦	✦	✦	✦	✦	✦		✦	✦
Know and apply grade-level phonics and word analysis skills in decoding words.	✦	✦	✦	✦	✦	✦	✦		✦	
Read with accuracy and fluency to support comprehension.	✦		✦	✦	✦	✦	✦	✦	✦	✦
Add details to strengthen writing.	✦		✦		✦					
Produce complete sentences.						✦	✦	✦		
Demonstrate command of the conventions of standard English grammar.	✦		✦		✦	✦	✦	✦		
Demonstrate command of capitalization, punctuation, and spelling.	✦		✦					✦	✦	✦
Determine the meaning of unknown and multiple-meaning words in a text.		✦	✦	✦		✦			✦	
Demonstrate understanding of figurative language, word relationships, and nuances in word meanings.								✦	✦	

Help Your Child Get Ready: Week 1

Here are some activities that you and your child might enjoy.

Sizzling Synonyms!

The first time your child says, "It's hot outside," challenge him or her to come up with as many words as possible that mean the same thing as *hot*. You can try this with other weather words such as *cold, rainy,* or *cloudy*.

Summer Goal

Suggest that your child come up with a plan to achieve a goal by the end of the summer. For example, he or she may wish to become an expert on a favorite animal or learn to count in another language. Help him or her map out a way to be successful. Periodically, check to see how your child is progressing.

Order, Order!

Play a ranking game. Choose three related items and ask your child to put them in order. Ask him or her to explain the choice. For example, if you chose *ice cube, snowball,* and *frozen lake,* your child might say *small, medium,* and *large; or cold, colder, coldest.*

Sun Safety

Talk about sun safety with your child. Ask him or her to write a list of ways to stay safe in the sun. Post it in a prominent place!

These are the skills your child will be working on this week.

Math
- addition and subtraction within 10
- measure lengths
- partition shapes into equal parts
- place value with regrouping

Reading
- identify key details

Phonics & Vocabulary
- recognize words with short *a*

Grammar & Writing
- sentence punctuation
- capitalization

Incentive Chart: Week 1

Week 1	Day 1	Day 2	Day 3	Day 4	Day 5
Put a sticker to show you completed each day's work.	☆ ☆	☆ ☆	☆ ☆	☆ ☆	☆ ☆

CONGRATULATIONS!

Wow! You did a great job this week!

This certificate is presented to:

_____

_____   _____
Date   Parent/Caregiver's Signature

Punctuation Power

Each sentence is missing a punctuation mark.
Draw a line to match each punctuation mark to a sentence.

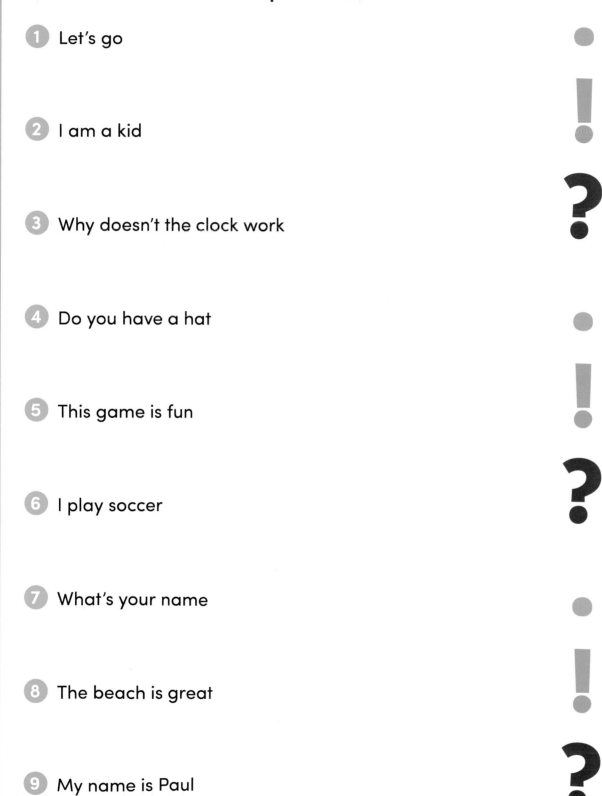

1. Let's go

2. I am a kid

3. Why doesn't the clock work

4. Do you have a hat

5. This game is fun

6. I play soccer

7. What's your name

8. The beach is great

9. My name is Paul

.

!

?

.

!

?

.

!

?

Shapes on a Snake

Write the number for each shape. Add or subtract.

1 ♥ + ⬭ = _____   6 ▱ − ◆ = _____

2 ⬭ − ⬣ = _____   7 ⬭ + ♥ = _____

3 ▭ + ⬣ = _____   8 ⬣ + ⬣ = _____

4 ◆ + ⬣ = _____   9 ♥ + ⬭ = _____

5 △ − ▭ = _____   10 ▱ − ⬣ = _____

Capitalizing Names and First Words

Read each sentence.
Fill in the circle next to the word that needs a capital letter.

1 i like the goat named Gruff.

○ Goats

○ The

○ I

2 I read the story with ron.

○ Read

○ Story

○ Ron

3 Little gruff had a problem.

○ Had

○ Gruff

○ Problem

4 troll was on the bridge.

○ On

○ Bridge

○ Troll

5 His name was nosey.

○ Name

○ Nosey

○ His

Tool Time

How many leaves long is each object? Write the answer on the line.

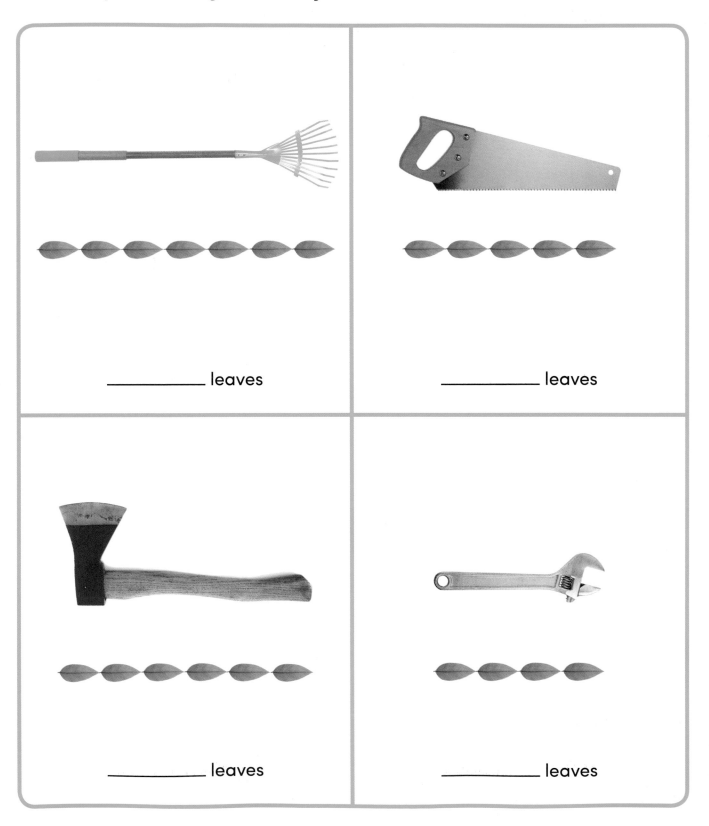

_____ leaves

_____ leaves

_____ leaves

_____ leaves

Hunt for Short *a*

Write the word for each picture. Use the Word Bank.
Then find and circle the words in the word search.

Word Bank

| apple | cat | ham | map | rat | van |

a	c	a	t	m
p	c	h	a	a
p	v	a	n	p
l	m	h	a	m
e	r	a	t	p

Look at the pictures in each box. Say the names.
X the picture in each box that does not have a short-*a* sound.

Make More Shapes

Follow the directions in each box below.

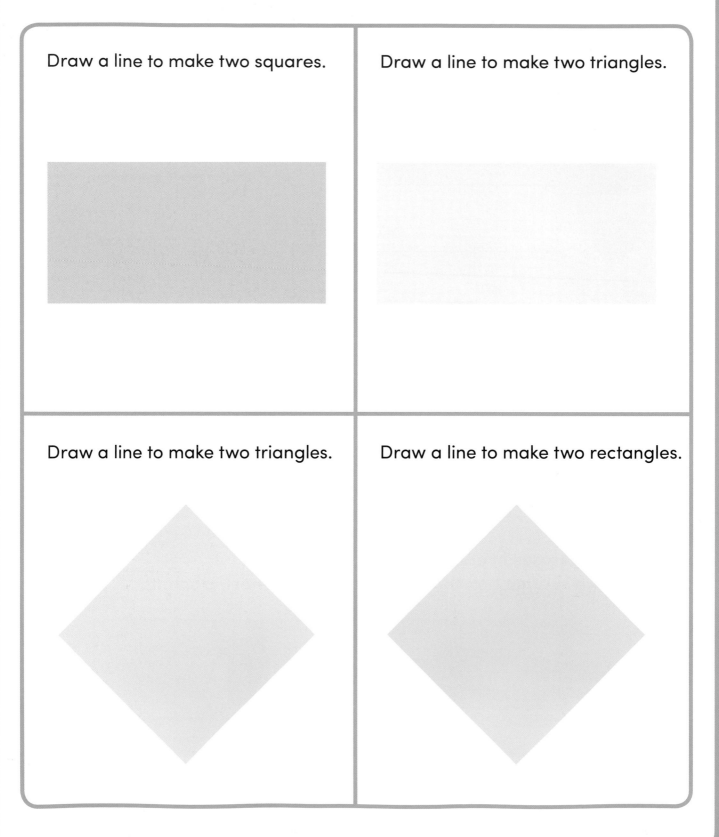

Draw a line to make two squares.

Draw a line to make two triangles.

Draw a line to make two triangles.

Draw a line to make two rectangles.

Big the Pig

**Read the story. Then answer each question.
Fill in the bubble next to the best answer.**

My name is Ted. I live in Texas. I have a pig. My pig's name is Big. Big lives in a pen. He plays in the mud. He eats apples and corn. Big is a very big pig!

1 Who is telling the story?

○ Big

○ Ted

○ Ted's friend

2 What does Ted have?

○ a dog

○ a pig

○ a cat

3 What is a good title (name) for this story?

○ Ted's Pig

○ Sam's Pig

○ Pig Pens

4 Write a sentence telling something about Big the pig.

_____

_____

_____

Solve the Riddle

Read the words and write the number. Solve the riddle using your answers.

two tens and ten ones	five tens and thirteen ones
_____ F	_____ I
four tens and sixteen ones	five tens and sixteen ones
_____ S	_____ M
two tens and fifteen ones	two tens and twenty ones
_____ E	_____ B
one ten and eighteen ones	seven tens and seventeen ones
_____ R	_____ A
eight tens and eleven ones	six tens and twelve ones
_____ N	_____ P

Write the letter that goes with each number.

What animal never tells the truth?

____ ____ - ____ ____ ____ - ____ ____ ____ ____
87   66   30   63   40   63   87   91   56

My Uncle's Airplane

Read the story. Then answer the questions.

My name is Bill. My favorite uncle George has a new airplane! It's white with red and blue stripes. It flies very high. He took me on a trip in his new plane. We went to the shore. The name of his plane is White Bird. I hope my uncle will take me on another trip soon.

1 Who has a new airplane?

_____

_____

2 Describe the airplane.

_____

_____

3 Who took a trip in the new airplane?

_____

_____

4 What is the name of the airplane?

_____

_____

Box of Chocolates

Cindy Chipmunk had 10 chocolates in each box of candy. She opened the boxes to taste the chocolates inside. Look at how many chocolates are in each box now. Then answer the question. Write an equation to show how you got your answer. The first one is done for you.

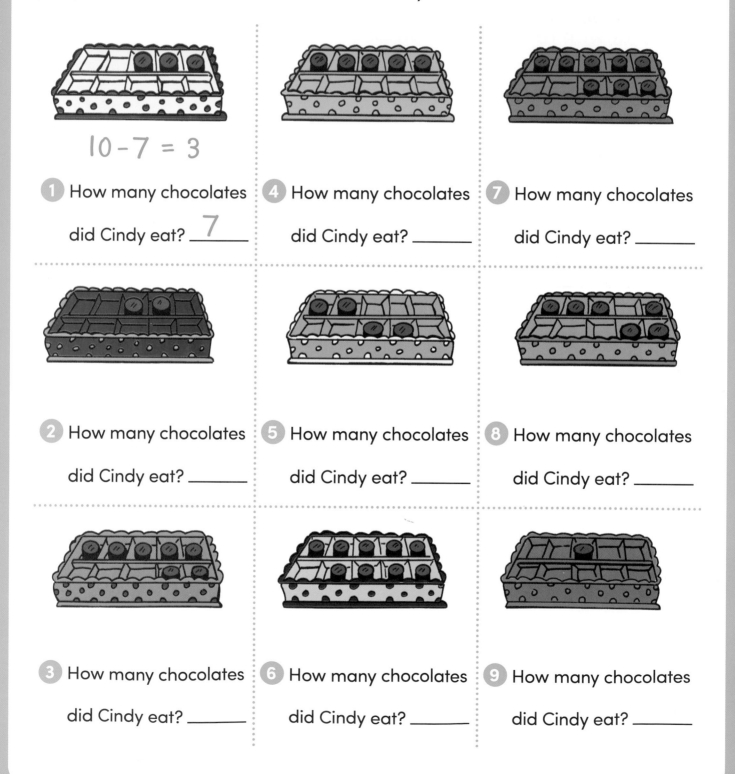

10 - 7 = 3

1 How many chocolates did Cindy eat? __7__

4 How many chocolates did Cindy eat? _____

7 How many chocolates did Cindy eat? _____

2 How many chocolates did Cindy eat? _____

5 How many chocolates did Cindy eat? _____

8 How many chocolates did Cindy eat? _____

3 How many chocolates did Cindy eat? _____

6 How many chocolates did Cindy eat? _____

9 How many chocolates did Cindy eat? _____

Help Your Child Get Ready: Week 2

Here are some activities that you and your child might enjoy.

Rainbow Hunt

Ask your child to find one object for each color of the rainbow: red, orange, yellow, green, blue, and purple.

Scrambled Names

Have your child write his or her first and last name on a sheet of paper and cut apart the letters. Encourage your child to use the letters to make new words. For variety, your child might also use the names of friends and family members.

Daily Timeline

Help your child practice sequencing by creating a timeline of the daily routine. Encourage him or her to draw pictures or write words to describe what happened first, next, and so on.

Find Your Way Home

Invite your child to make a map of your neighborhood. He or she can draw and label what is in front, behind, to the left, and to the right of your home.

These are the skills your child will be working on this week.

Math

- understand tens and ones through 19
- addition within 20
- recognize numbers and number words through 100
- compare numbers
- tell time

Reading

- compare and contrast
- context clues

Phonics & Vocabulary

- digraph *th*
- recognize words with short *e*
- identify syllables
- recognize words with short *i*

Incentive Chart: Week 2

Week 2	Day 1	Day 2	Day 3	Day 4	Day 5
Put a sticker to show you completed each day's work.	☆ ☆	☆ ☆	☆ ☆	☆ ☆	☆ ☆

CONGRATULATIONS!

Wow! You did a great job this week!

This certificate is presented to:

_____

_____   _____
Date   Parent/Caregiver's Signature

Those Thorns!

The letters **th** make the sound at the beginning of the word *thorn*.

Read the words in the Word Bank. Circle the letters **th** in each word. Use the words to complete the lists below.

Word Bank

the	this	with	then
bath	that	moth	they

Words that begin with th.

_____

_____

_____

_____

_____

Words that end with th.

_____

_____

_____

_____

_____

Choose a word from the Word Bank that rhymes with each word.

1 path _____

2 hen _____

3 rat _____

Unscramble each word.

4 het _____

5 hiwt _____

6 tsih _____

Tens and Ones

Write the number that is shown.

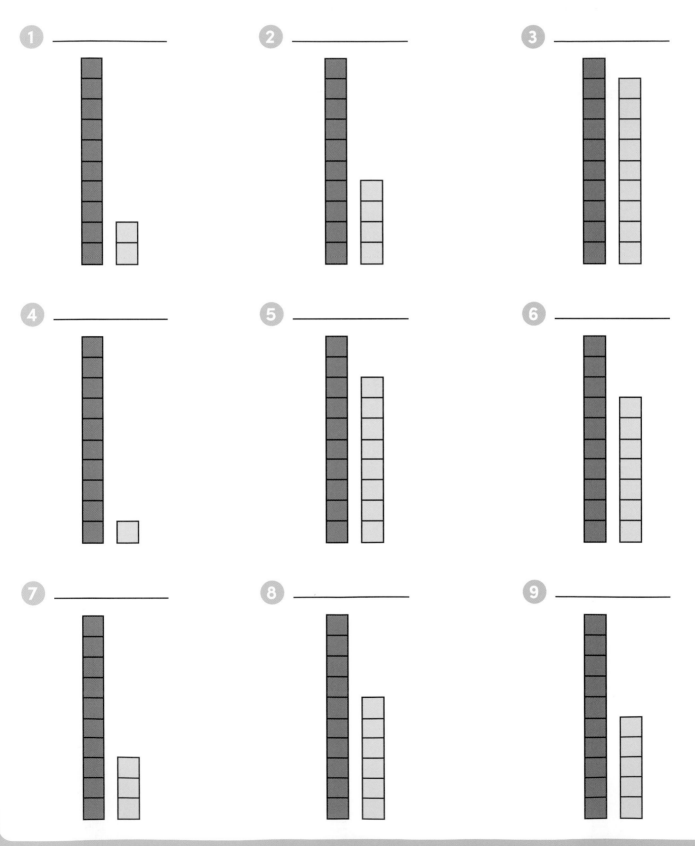

1 _____

2 _____

3 _____

4 _____

5 _____

6 _____

7 _____

8 _____

9 _____

Hunt for Short e

Write the word for each picture. Use the Word Bank.
Then find and circle the words in the word search.

Word Bank

| bed | dress | egg | nest | ten | web |

_____

_____

_____

_____

_____

_____

w	e	b	k	d
n	e	e	b	r
e	g	c	e	e
s	g	r	d	s
t	t	e	n	s

Look at the picture. Fill in the circle
next to the sentence that tells about
the picture.

○ This room is a mess!

○ His room is a map!

Crack the Code!

Solve these math problems. Use your answers to solve the riddle below.

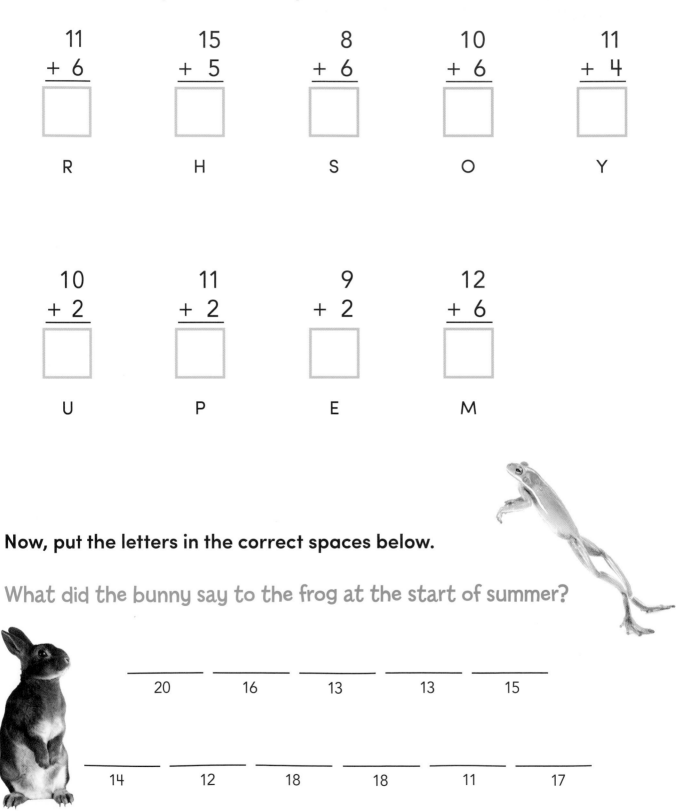

$$\begin{array}{r} 11 \\ + 6 \\ \hline \end{array}$$
☐
R

$$\begin{array}{r} 15 \\ + 5 \\ \hline \end{array}$$
☐
H

$$\begin{array}{r} 8 \\ + 6 \\ \hline \end{array}$$
☐
S

$$\begin{array}{r} 10 \\ + 6 \\ \hline \end{array}$$
☐
O

$$\begin{array}{r} 11 \\ + 4 \\ \hline \end{array}$$
☐
Y

$$\begin{array}{r} 10 \\ + 2 \\ \hline \end{array}$$
☐
U

$$\begin{array}{r} 11 \\ + 2 \\ \hline \end{array}$$
☐
P

$$\begin{array}{r} 9 \\ + 2 \\ \hline \end{array}$$
☐
E

$$\begin{array}{r} 12 \\ + 6 \\ \hline \end{array}$$
☐
M

Now, put the letters in the correct spaces below.

What did the bunny say to the frog at the start of summer?

___ ___ ___ ___ ___
20   16   13   13   15

___ ___ ___ ___ ___ ___
14   12   18   18   11   17

Syllable Match

Look at each picture. Say the word.
Fill in the circle that tells how many syllables.

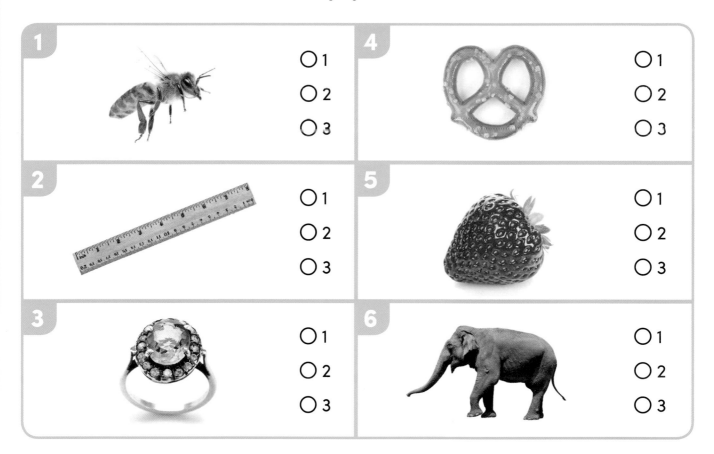

1. ○ 1 ○ 2 ○ 3
2. ○ 1 ○ 2 ○ 3
3. ○ 1 ○ 2 ○ 3
4. ○ 1 ○ 2 ○ 3
5. ○ 1 ○ 2 ○ 3
6. ○ 1 ○ 2 ○ 3

Say the name for each picture.
X the picture in each section that does not match the number of syllables.

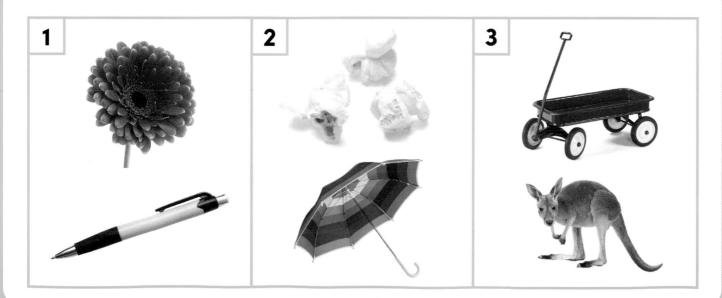

Number Match

Draw a line to match each number word to its number.

twenty-five

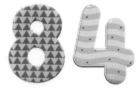

thirty-six

fifteen

forty

sixty-one

one hundred

ninety-three

six

fifty-five

eighty-four

twelve

forty-two

Hunt for Short *i*

Write the word for each picture. Use the Word Bank.
Then find and circle the words in the word search.

Word Bank

| fish | milk | pin | ship | six | zip |

_____

_____

_____

_____

_____

f	s	i	x	m
i	z	a	p	i
s	i	w	i	l
h	p	r	n	k
s	h	i	p	s

Say the name for each picture.
X the pictures that do not have the short-*i* sound.

Greater Than or Less Than?

Compare the numbers. Use the number line.
Write > or < in each number sentence.

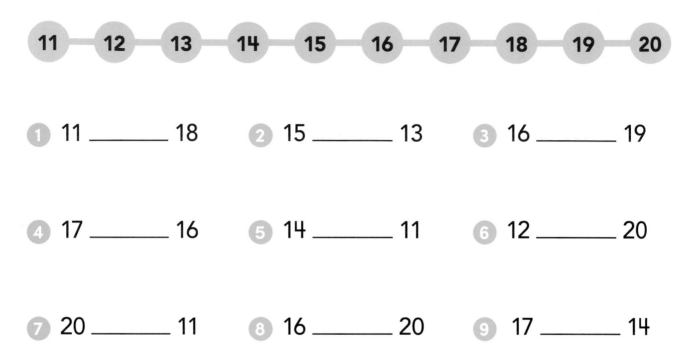

11　12　13　14　15　16　17　18　19　20

1 11 _____ 18

2 15 _____ 13

3 16 _____ 19

4 17 _____ 16

5 14 _____ 11

6 12 _____ 20

7 20 _____ 11

8 16 _____ 20

9 17 _____ 14

10 Circle the **3rd** grape.

11 Circle the **5th** grape.

Life in the Ocean

Read about life in the ocean. Then answer the questions.

Dolphins live in the wide, open sea. They **roam** the ocean to catch fish. Dolphins do not swim too deep. They must come up to breathe.

Dolphins

Anglerfish live in the deep dark sea. They make their own light with a light pole. The light pole grows on top of their head! What happens when other fish swim toward the light? The anglerfish catches them!

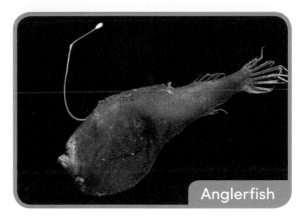
Anglerfish

1 How are dolphins and anglerfish alike?
   ○ Both live in the sea.
   ○ Both have a light pole.
   ○ Both need to breathe air.

2 How are anglerfish and dolphins different?
   ○ Anglerfish eat fish.
   ○ Anglerfish live in the deep sea.
   ○ Dolphins can swim.

3 In the first paragraph, the word **roam** means
   ○ part of a home.
   ○ look for.
   ○ move from place to place.

Ready for Bed

Draw a line to match the clocks on the cat with the digital clocks.

Help Your Child Get Ready: Week 3

Here are some activities that you and your child might enjoy.

Silly Summer Sentences

How can summer turn into a tongue twister? Guide your child to make up a sentence using the word *summer* and as many other words as possible that start with *s*.

What's Your Estimate?

Ask your child to estimate how many times in 60 seconds he or she can say "Mississippi" or write his or her name. Then have him or her try the activity and compare the results with the estimate.

Words Can Add Up

Assign a monetary value to words. For example, a consonant can be worth one penny and a vowel can be worth one nickel. Challenge your child to find a word with a high value.

Room With a View

Invite your child to look out of a window. Have your child describe or draw 10 things in the scene. Remind him or her to use lots of detail.

These are the skills your child will be working on this week.

Math

- measure lengths
- number sequence through 120
- understand place value
- subtraction within 6
- solve word problems
- use a number line to add
- commutative property of addition

Reading

- differentiate between fact and fiction

Phonics & Vocabulary

- digraph *sh*
- recognize words with short *o*

Grammar & Writing

- use plurals
- possessive nouns

Incentive Chart: Week 3

Week 3	Day 1	Day 2	Day 3	Day 4	Day 5
Put a sticker to show you completed each day's work.	☆ ☆	☆ ☆	☆ ☆	☆ ☆	☆ ☆

CONGRATULATIONS!

Wow! You did a great job this week!

This certificate is presented to:

_____

_____   _____
Date   Parent/Caregiver's Signature

Field Trip

Take a field trip to a farm! Say the name for each picture. Circle the word that matches each picture, then write it. Tell a story about the field trip.

bus   buses

_____

puppies   puppy

_____

chicks   chick

_____

lamb   lambs

_____

Look at the picture. Fill in the missing letters. Use the Letter Bank. Read the sentence.

Letter Bank

s   es

The kitten_____ are sitting in their dish_____ _____!

Silly Snake

How many inches long is each snake? Write the answer.

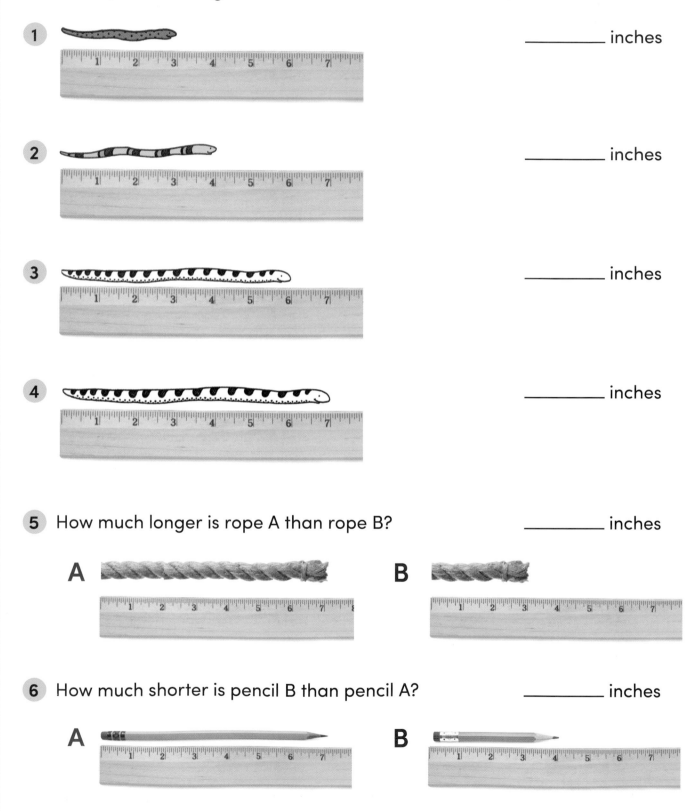

1 _____ inches

2 _____ inches

3 _____ inches

4 _____ inches

5 How much longer is rope A than rope B? _____ inches

A   B

6 How much shorter is pencil B than pencil A? _____ inches

A   B

Shiny Shells

The letters **sh** make the sound at the beginning of the word *shell*.

Read the words in the Word Bank. Circle the letters **sh** in each word. Use the words to complete the lists below.

Word Bank

ship	she	fish	shape
wish	brush	shine	shoe

Words that begin with sh.

_____

_____

_____

_____

_____

Words that end with sh.

_____

_____

_____

_____

_____

Circle the word that is spelled correctly.

1 shipe   ship

2 shape   shap

3 she   shee

4 fish   fich

5 brosh   brush

6 wich   wish

I Can Count to 120!

This chart is missing some numbers. Fill in the missing numbers.

1	2	3	4	5					
					16	17	18	19	20
21	22	23	24	25					
					36	37	38	39	40
41	42	43	44	45					
					56	57	58	59	60
61	62	63	64	65					
					76	77	78	79	80
81	82	83	84	85					
					96	97	98	99	100
101	102	103	104	105					
					116	117	118	119	120

Hunt for Short o

Write the word for each picture. Use the Word Bank.
Then find and circle the words in the word search.

Word Bank

| box | doll | fox | sock | stop | top |

_____

_____

_____

_____

_____

_____

s	o	c	k	t
s	b	o	x	d
t	f	t	b	o
o	o	o	d	l
p	x	p	p	l

Say the name for each picture.
X the pictures that do not have the short-o sound.

Mixed Math

Draw lines to make matches.

1 ten 0 ones •   • 13   1 ten 5 ones •   • 18

1 ten 1 one •   • 14   1 ten 6 ones •   • 15

1 ten 2 ones •   • 11   1 ten 7 ones •   • 19

1 ten 3 ones •   • 12   1 ten 8 ones •   • 16

1 ten 4 ones •   • 10   1 ten 9 ones •   • 17

Fast Practice
Subtract.

6 – 1 = _____   5 – 2 = _____   4 – 3 = _____

5 – 3 = _____   4 – 2 = _____   6 – 2 = _____

Solve It!
Read each sentence. Draw and label the children from tallest to shortest.

Kim is shorter than Rob.   Max is taller than Rob.   Max is taller than Kim.

Whose Is It?

A **noun** can show who owns something. This is done by adding an (') and **s**.

Joe is going on a trip. He needs to pack everything on his list. Each object belongs to a different family member.

Study the picture to learn who owns each item. Write it on the suitcase. The first one is done for you.

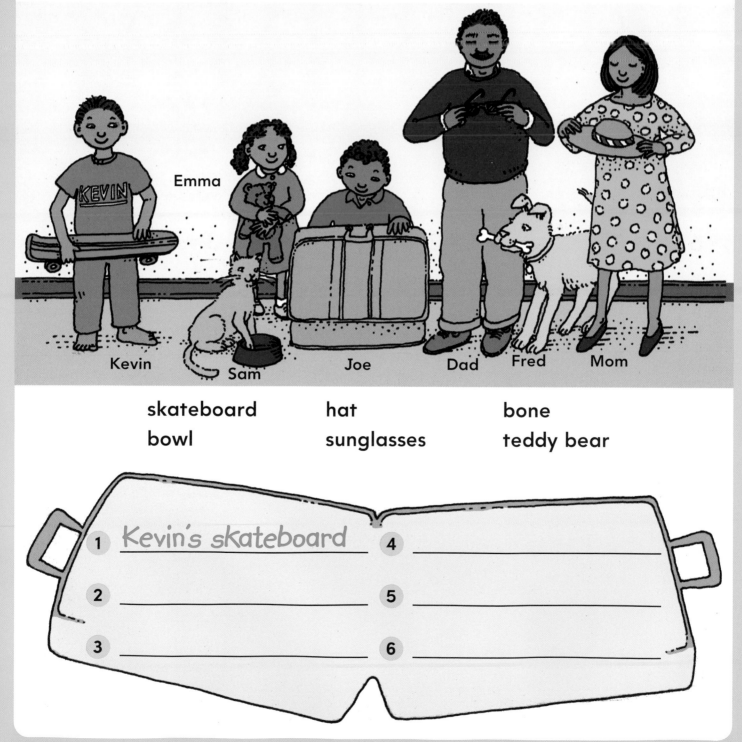

skateboard   hat   bone
bowl   sunglasses   teddy bear

1   Kevin's skateboard   4   _____

2   _____   5   _____

3   _____   6   _____

Use a Number Line

Find the sum. Use the number line to help you.

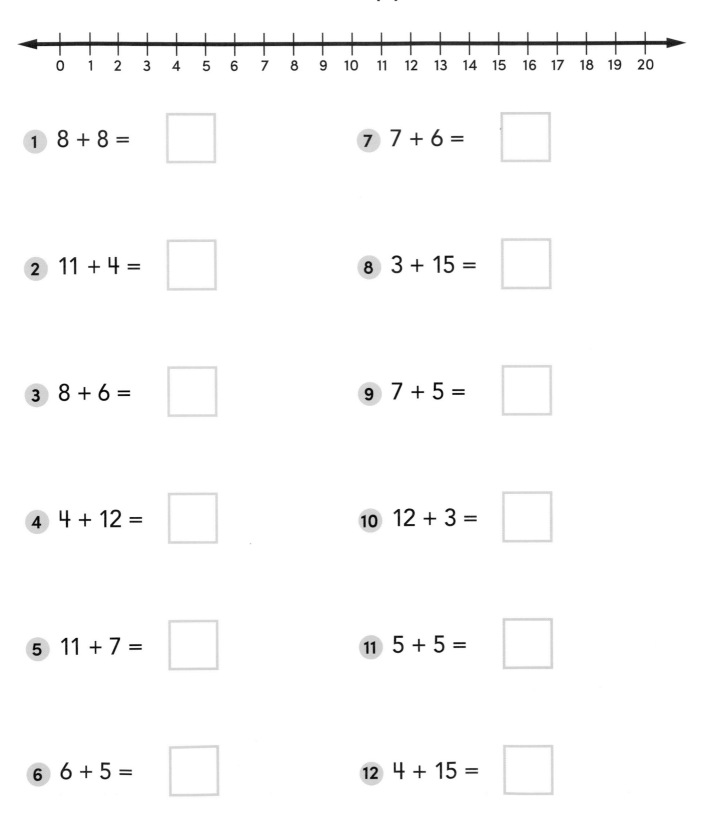

1 8 + 8 =

2 11 + 4 =

3 8 + 6 =

4 4 + 12 =

5 11 + 7 =

6 6 + 5 =

7 7 + 6 =

8 3 + 15 =

9 7 + 5 =

10 12 + 3 =

11 5 + 5 =

12 4 + 15 =

Fact or Fiction

Read the story. Then answer the questions.

This morning, Max took a boat ride on the sea. On his way home, a big wave tipped the boat over. Max fell out.

Max was scared. He could not swim. Soon he saw a mermaid. The mermaid saved Max. Max met her friend Dolphin. Then, she took Max to her sea cave. She showed Max her pet starfish.

1 When did Max take a boat trip?

   ○ in the morning
   ○ in the afternoon

2 Why was Max afraid?

   ○ He was afraid of the water.
   ○ He could not swim.

3 Who saved Max?

   ○ A mermaid saved Max.
   ○ A boat saved Max.

4 How do you know that the story is fiction? _____

_____

What's the Missing Sum?

Find the missing sum. Use the commutative property.

1 $3 + 5 = 8$

$5 + 3 = $ _____

2 $7 + 2 = 9$

$2 + 7 = $ _____

3 $5 + 2 = 7$

$2 + 5 = $ _____

4 $1 + 3 = 4$

$3 + 1 = $ _____

5 $4 + 5 = 9$

$5 + 4 = $ _____

6 $4 + 1 = 5$

$1 + 4 = $ _____

7 $1 + 2 = 3$

$2 + 1 = $ _____

8 $4 + 2 = 6$

$2 + 4 = $ _____

9 $2 + 3 = 5$

$3 + 2 = $ _____

10 $1 + 7 = 8$

$7 + 1 = $ _____

Help Your Child Get Ready: Week 4

Here are some activities that you and your child might enjoy.

Starring Role

All children like to hear stories about themselves. Help your child feel like a star by sharing memories of him or her, finding stories with characters that have your child's name, or when reading aloud to your child, insert his or her name in place of the main character's.

Compound Interest

Point out examples of compound words to your child. Then have him or her keep track of the compound words heard during an hour. Try it another time and challenge your child to improve on his or her last "score."

The Case of the Mysterious Sock

Invite your child to find a secret object to put in a sock. Try to guess what it is by feeling the object through the sock. Trade roles. Play again.

Start Collecting

Having a collection is a great way for a child to develop higher-level thinking skills like sorting and analyzing. Encourage your child to start one. Leaves, rocks, stamps, or shells are all easy and fun things to collect.

These are the skills your child will be working on this week.

Math

- addition within 50
- subtraction within 18
- use a number line to add three numbers
- understand place value
- solve word problems

Reading

- identify the main idea
- context clues

Phonics & Vocabulary

- short-*u* words
- vowel teams: *ai, ay*
- homonyms
- long-*a* and long-*i* words

Incentive Chart: Week 4

Week 4	Day 1	Day 2	Day 3	Day 4	Day 5
Put a sticker to show you completed each day's work.	☆ ☆	☆ ☆	☆ ☆	☆ ☆	☆ ☆

CONGRATULATIONS!

Wow! You did a great job this week!

This certificate is presented to:

_____

_____ _____
Date   Parent/Caregiver's Signature

Hunt for Short *u*

Write the word for each picture. Use the Word Bank.
Then find and circle the words in the word search.

Word Bank

bug	bus	drum	rug	skunk	sun

_____

_____

_____

_____

_____

_____

b	u	g	d	r
b	s	b	r	u
u	u	e	u	g
s	n	c	m	v
s	k	u	n	k

Say the name for each picture.
X the pictures that do not have the short-*u* sound.

Kickboard Match Up

Add or subtract. Draw a line to match kickboards with the same answer.

Play Time

It's time to play! Say the name for each picture.
Circle the word, then write it. Use the words to tell a story.

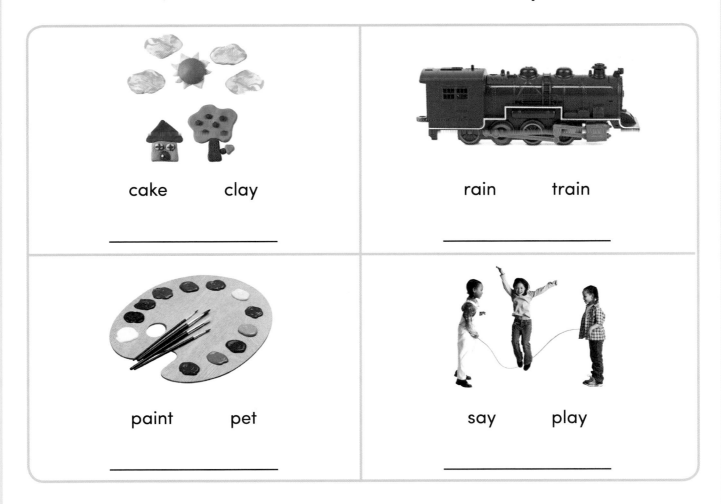

cake   clay

_____

rain   train

_____

paint   pet

_____

say   play

_____

Look at the picture. Fill in the missing letters.
Use the Letter Bank. Read the sentence.

Letter Bank

a   i   a   y

It's fun to pl____ ____

in the r____ ____n!

Penguin Parade

Add or subtract.

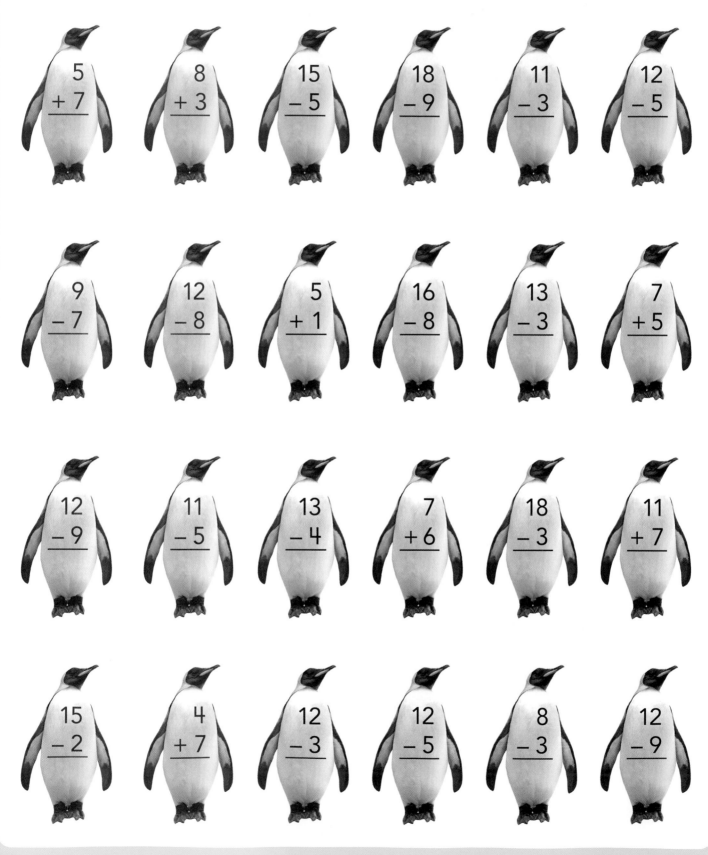

$$5 + 7$$

$$8 + 3$$

$$15 - 5$$

$$18 - 9$$

$$11 - 3$$

$$12 - 5$$

$$9 - 7$$

$$12 - 8$$

$$5 + 1$$

$$16 - 8$$

$$13 - 3$$

$$7 + 5$$

$$12 - 9$$

$$11 - 5$$

$$13 - 4$$

$$7 + 6$$

$$18 - 3$$

$$11 + 7$$

$$15 - 2$$

$$4 + 7$$

$$12 - 3$$

$$12 - 5$$

$$8 - 3$$

$$12 - 9$$

Multiple-Meaning Words

Complete each sentence with a word from the balloon that can be used in both blanks in each sentence. The first one is done for you.

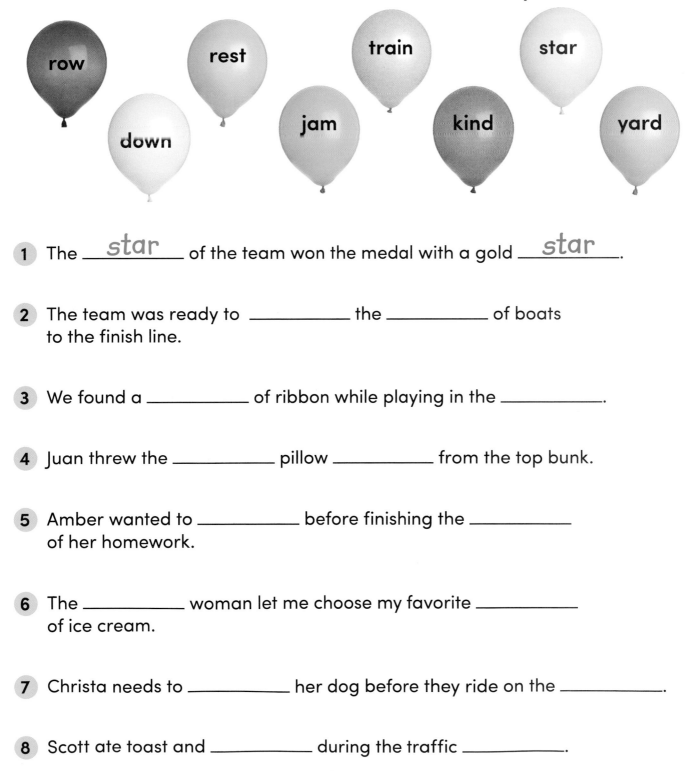

row   rest   train   star   down   jam   kind   yard

1. The ___star___ of the team won the medal with a gold ___star___.

2. The team was ready to _____ the _____ of boats to the finish line.

3. We found a _____ of ribbon while playing in the _____.

4. Juan threw the _____ pillow _____ from the top bunk.

5. Amber wanted to _____ before finishing the _____ of her homework.

6. The _____ woman let me choose my favorite _____ of ice cream.

7. Christa needs to _____ her dog before they ride on the _____.

8. Scott ate toast and _____ during the traffic _____.

Using a Number Line

Find the sum. Use the number line to help you.

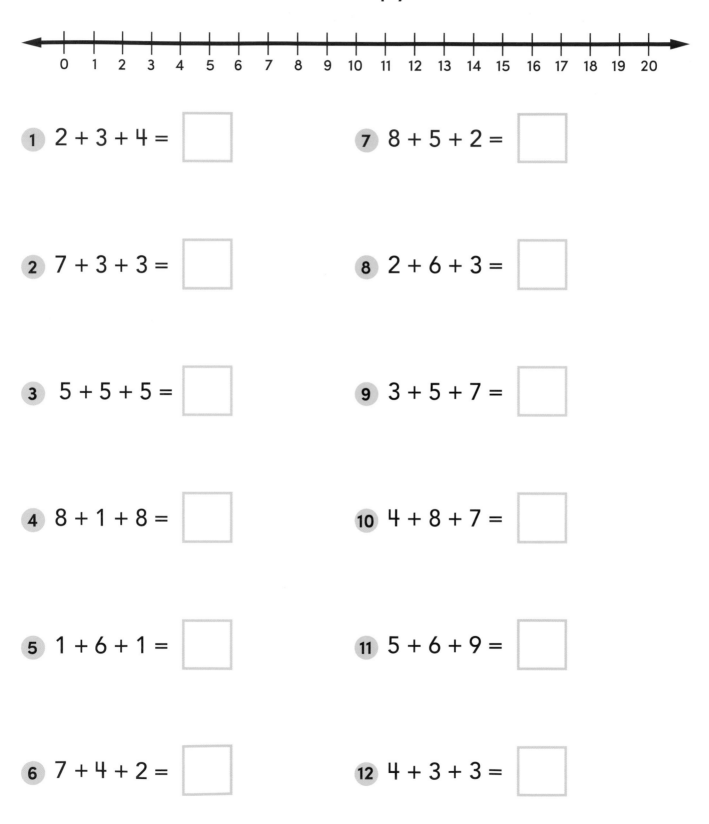

1 $2 + 3 + 4 =$ ☐

2 $7 + 3 + 3 =$ ☐

3 $5 + 5 + 5 =$ ☐

4 $8 + 1 + 8 =$ ☐

5 $1 + 6 + 1 =$ ☐

6 $7 + 4 + 2 =$ ☐

7 $8 + 5 + 2 =$ ☐

8 $2 + 6 + 3 =$ ☐

9 $3 + 5 + 7 =$ ☐

10 $4 + 8 + 7 =$ ☐

11 $5 + 6 + 9 =$ ☐

12 $4 + 3 + 3 =$ ☐

Hunt for Long *a* and Long *i*

Write the word for each picture. Use the Word Bank.
Then find and circle the words in the word search.

Word Bank

| bike | five | mice | rake | skate | whale |

_____

_____

_____

_____

_____

_____

m	i	c	e	r	w
s	f	i	v	e	h
k	r	t	s	o	a
a	r	a	k	e	l
t	w	d	f	c	e
e	b	b	i	k	e

Say the word for each picture. Write *A* for the long-*a* sound.
Write *I* for the long-*i* sound.

_____   _____   _____   _____

Mixed Math

How many tens are in each number? How many ones are there?
Write your answer on the lines. The first one is done for you.

26 = __2__ tens 6 ones   54 = 5 tens _____ ones

47 = _____ tens 7 ones   82 = 8 tens _____ ones

39 = _____ tens 9 ones   75 = 7 tens _____ ones

Fast Practice
Subtract. Think **about doubles.**

10 – 5 = _____   8 – 4 = _____   6 – 3 = _____

6 – _____ = 3   4 – _____ = 2   14 – _____ = 7

Solve It!
Libby has a nickel. Then she finds 2 pennies.
How much money does Libby have now?

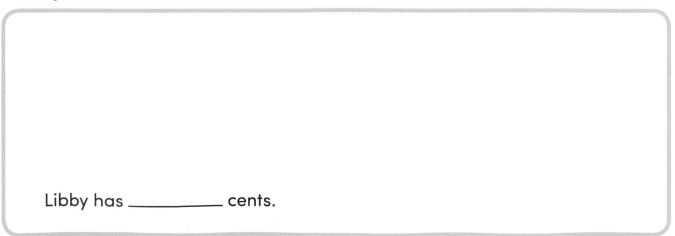

Show your work.

Libby has _____ cents.

The Biggest Spoon

Read the paragraph.
Then answer the questions.

What is the biggest spoon in the world? It is a group of bright stars called the Big Dipper. On a **clear** night, look up at the sky. The Big Dipper might be right side up. It might be upside down! People can use the Big Dipper to find their way when they get lost.

1 What is the main idea of this paragraph?
○ The Big Dipper is a group of stars.
○ You need a big spoon to eat.
○ The Big Dipper may be upside down.

2 You can guess that the Big Dipper is
○ hard to see in fog.
○ easy to see in the sun.
○ easy to see indoors.

3 In this paragraph, the word **clear** means
○ dark.
○ rainy.
○ not cloudy.

Little Pig's Problem

Little Pig has a big problem! His homework got crushed in his book bag, and now he can't read it.

To help Little Pig fix his homework, find each missing number. Then write the number in the box.

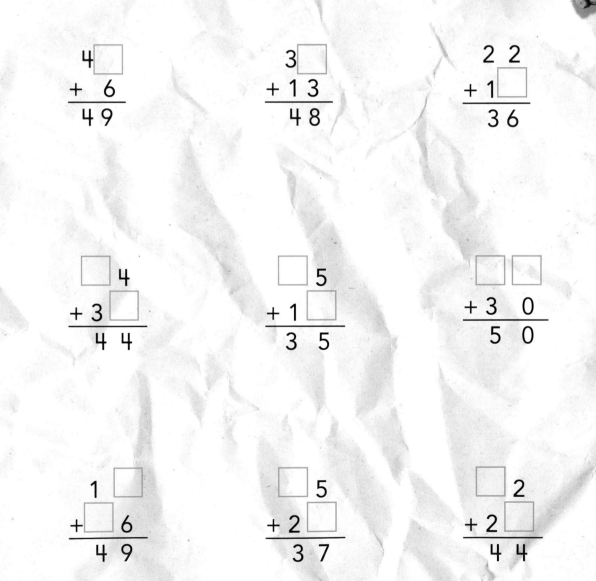

$$\begin{array}{r} 4\,\square \\ +\ 6 \\ \hline 4\ 9 \end{array} \qquad \begin{array}{r} 3\,\square \\ +\ 1\ 3 \\ \hline 4\ 8 \end{array} \qquad \begin{array}{r} 2\ 2 \\ +\ 1\,\square \\ \hline 3\ 6 \end{array}$$

$$\begin{array}{r} \square\ 4 \\ +\ 3\,\square \\ \hline 4\ 4 \end{array} \qquad \begin{array}{r} \square\ 5 \\ +\ 1\,\square \\ \hline 3\ 5 \end{array} \qquad \begin{array}{r} \square\ \square \\ +\ 3\ 0 \\ \hline 5\ 0 \end{array}$$

$$\begin{array}{r} 1\,\square \\ +\,\square\ 6 \\ \hline 4\ 9 \end{array} \qquad \begin{array}{r} \square\ 5 \\ +\ 2\,\square \\ \hline 3\ 7 \end{array} \qquad \begin{array}{r} \square\ 2 \\ +\ 2\,\square \\ \hline 4\ 4 \end{array}$$

Help Your Child Get Ready: Week 5

Here are some activities that you and your child might enjoy.

Word Chain

Develop your child's listening skills by playing "Word Chain." In this game, someone says a word, and the next person must say a word that begins with the last letter of the previous player's word.

Connecting Words

Give your child a word and encourage him or her to tell you the thing that often goes with it, such as peanut butter (and jelly) or thunder (and lightning). Or, make analogy pairs such as finger and hand (and toe and foot). Playing word association games can help your child build vocabulary by making connections between words.

Fruit Kebabs

Your child can practice patterning by creating a tasty snack. Using a small wooden skewer and a selection of three different fruits, such as grapes, strawberries, and banana slices, invite your child to create a pattern with the fruit. Encourage your child to describe the pattern to you, or suggest a pattern for your child to use, such as *ABCABC* or *ABACABAC*.

Now You See It, Now You Don't

Show your child an interesting picture and ask him or her to look at it for a minute. Then turn the picture over and ask your child to list the objects that he or she can remember on a sheet of paper. If you wish, allow your child to look at the picture for another minute to help him or her add more items to the list.

These are the skills your child will be working on this week.

Math
- understand tens and ones in larger numbers
- compare lengths and heights
- add 1- and 2-digit numbers
- interpret data in a graph
- draw symmetrical shapes

Reading
- compare and contrast

Phonics & Vocabulary
- recognize words with long *o* and long *u*
- digraphs: *ch, wh*

Grammar & Writing
- past-tense verbs
- inflections: *-ing, -ed*

Incentive Chart: Week 5

Week 5	Day 1	Day 2	Day 3	Day 4	Day 5
Put a sticker to show you completed each day's work.	☆ ☆	☆ ☆	☆ ☆	☆ ☆	☆ ☆

CONGRATULATIONS!

Wow! You did a great job this week!

This certificate is presented to:

_____

_____   _____
Date   Parent/Caregiver's Signature

What Happened?

Some **verbs** add *-ed* to tell about actions that happened in the past.

Read the first sentence in each pair.
Change the underlined verb to tell about the past.

1 Today, my dogs <u>push</u> open the back door.

Yesterday, my dogs _____ open the back door.

2 Today, they <u>splash</u> in the rain puddles.

Last night, they _____ in the rain puddles.

3 Now, they <u>roll</u> in the mud.

Last week, they _____ in the mud.

4 Today, I <u>follow</u> my dogs' footprints.

Last Sunday, I _____ my dogs' footprints.

5 Now, I <u>wash</u> my dogs from head to toe.

Earlier, I _____ my dogs from head to toe.

Write a sentence using one of the verbs you wrote.

_____

_____

_____

_____

Tens and Ones

Write the number that is shown.

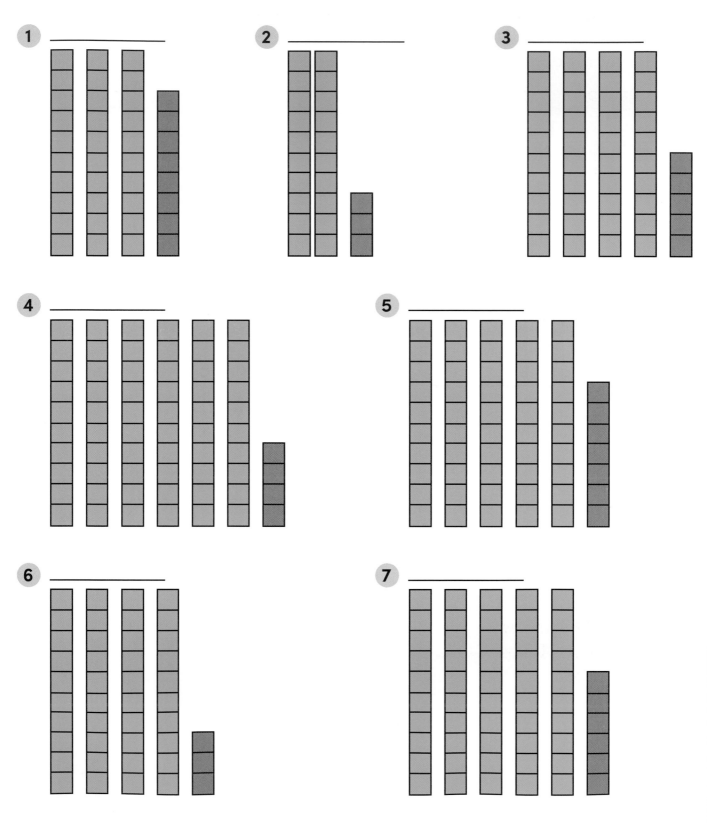

1 _____

2 _____

3 _____

4 _____

5 _____

6 _____

7 _____

Hunt for Long *o* and Long *u*

Write the word for each picture. Use the Word Bank.
Then find and circle the words in the word search.

Word Bank

bone	cone	cube	mule	nose	rose

_____

_____

_____

_____

_____

_____

r	c	o	n	e	e
o	m	u	l	e	c
s	u	m	n	o	u
e	l	o	n	s	b
v	n	o	s	e	e
o	b	o	n	e	b

What is a word that tells about
the puppy? Fill in the missing
letters. Use the Letter Bank.
Read the word.

Letter Bank

e	u

c _____ t _____

In Real Life . . .

Put on your thinking cap and circle each answer.

1 In real life, which one is the longest?

2 In real life, which one is the tallest?

Why Change?

Read the words in the Word Bank.
Circle the letters **ch** and **wh** in each word.
Use the words to complete the lists below.

The letters **ch** make the sound at the beginning of the word *chain*.

The letters **wh** make the sound at the beginning of the word *wheel*.

Word Bank

chin	chop	whale	when
inch	which	why	what

Words that start with **ch**.	Words that end with **ch**.	Words that start with **wh**.
_____	_____	_____
_____	_____	_____
_____	_____	_____
_____	_____	_____
_____	_____	_____

Write the word from the Word Bank that rhymes with each word below.

1 tail _____

2 mop _____

3 pinch _____

4 pitch _____

5 pen _____

6 win _____

Adding Numbers

Find the sum. Use the hundreds chart to help you.

1	2	3	4	5	6	7	8	9	10
11	12	13	14	15	16	17	18	19	20
21	22	23	24	25	26	27	28	29	30
31	32	33	34	35	36	37	38	39	40
41	42	43	44	45	46	47	48	49	50
51	52	53	54	55	56	57	58	59	60
61	62	63	64	65	66	67	68	69	70
71	72	73	74	75	76	77	78	79	80
81	82	83	84	85	86	87	88	89	90
91	92	93	94	95	96	97	98	99	100

1 $14 + 5 =$ _____

2 $11 + 5 =$ _____

3 $27 + 8 =$ _____

4 $41 + 8 =$ _____

5 $64 + 6 =$ _____

6 $81 + 7 =$ _____

7 $15 + 6 =$ _____

8 $22 + 6 =$ _____

9 $35 + 7 =$ _____

10 $56 + 9 =$ _____

11 $73 + 9 =$ _____

12 $93 + 6 =$ _____

What an End!

Add -ing and -ed to each base word in the chart. One row is done for you.

Base Word	-ing	-ed
1 show	showing	showed
2 lick		
3 plant		
4 brush		
5 walk		
6 play		

**Complete each sentence. Use a word from the chart above.
The first one is done for you.**

7 Yesterday, I _____ planted _____ two new trees.

8 Earlier, I _____ Martha my bike.

9 Today, I am _____ with Jake and Will.

10 Earlier this morning, I _____ to Grandma's.

See Our Seashells

Use the graph to answer the questions.

Seashells We Found

Ming	**Danny**	**Eva**	**Jack**

1 How many children found shells? _____

2 How many shells did the children find in all? _____

3 Who found the fewest shells? _____

4 Two children found 4 shells each. Write their names.

_____ and _____

5 Who found the most shells? _____

Twins

Holly and Polly are twins. They are in the first grade. They look alike, but they are very different. Holly likes to play softball and soccer. She likes to wear her hair braided when she goes out to play. She wears sporty clothes. Recess is her favorite part of school. Polly likes to read books and paint pictures. Every day she wears a ribbon in her hair to match her dress. Her favorite thing about school is going to the library. She wants to be a teacher some day.

Look at the pictures of Holly and Polly. They look alike but there are differences. Can you find them? Circle the things that are different.

Underline the sentence that tells what is the same about Holly and Polly.

They play sports.　　　They love to paint.　　　They are in the first grade.

Complete the Shape

Draw the other half of each shape. Example:

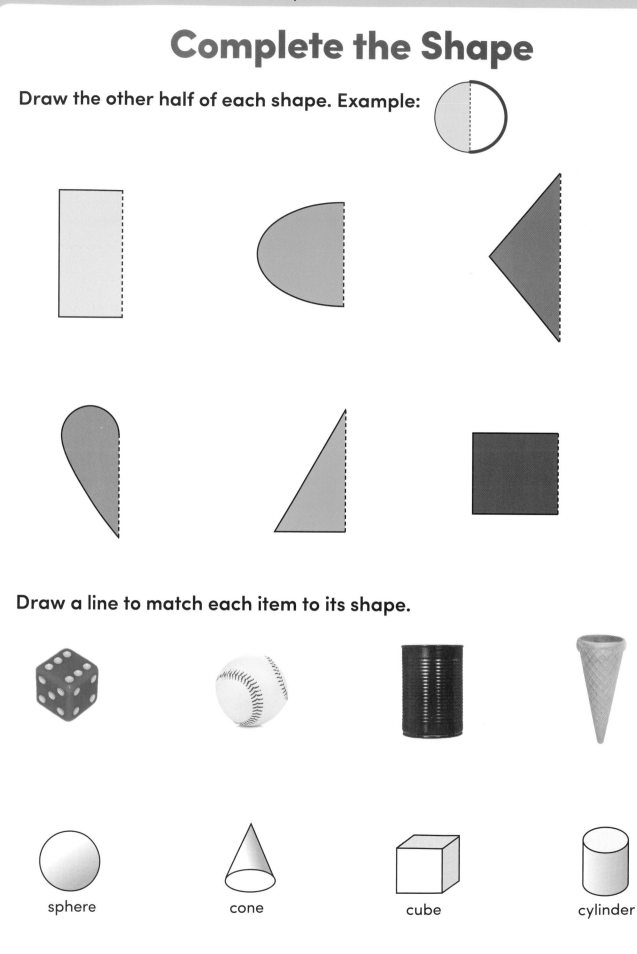

Draw a line to match each item to its shape.

sphere   cone   cube   cylinder

Help Your Child Get Ready: Week 6

Here are some activities that you and your child might enjoy.

What's in the Bag?

Before putting groceries away, have your child sort the items into categories and explain why he or she decided to group things in a certain way. This activity will help your child understand similarities and differences, as well as exercise descriptive skills.

What's in a Label?

Show examples of food labels to your child. Can he or she find a picture and some numbers on the label? Ask: *What do they tell you?*

Two's Company

Ask your child to look around and find things that come in a group, such as twos, fives, or tens.

Shopping List Maker

Invite your child to become your official shopping list maker. Dictate to him or her all the items you'll need to purchase on your next trip to the grocery store. This is a great way to build spelling skills.

These are the skills your child will be working on this week.

Math
- measure lengths
- tell time
- compare numbers
- addition sentences
- commutative property of addition

Reading
- use text features
- identify main idea and details

Phonics & Vocabulary
- vowel teams: *ea, ee, oa, oe, ow*
- position words

Grammar & Writing
- inflections: *–ed, –ing*

Incentive Chart: Week 6

Week 6	Day 1	Day 2	Day 3	Day 4	Day 5
Put a sticker to show you completed each day's work.	☆ ☆	☆ ☆	☆ ☆	☆ ☆	☆ ☆

CONGRATULATIONS!

Wow! You did a great job this week!

This certificate is presented to:

_____

_____ _____
Date   Parent/Caregiver's Signature

In the Garden

What's growing in this garden? Say the name for each picture.
Circle the word, then write it. Use the words to tell a story.

seeds   sent

_____

bees   beans

_____

peas   pet

_____

books   beets

_____

Look at the picture. Fill in the missing letters.
Use the Letter Bank. Read the sentence.

Letter Bank

g   e   a

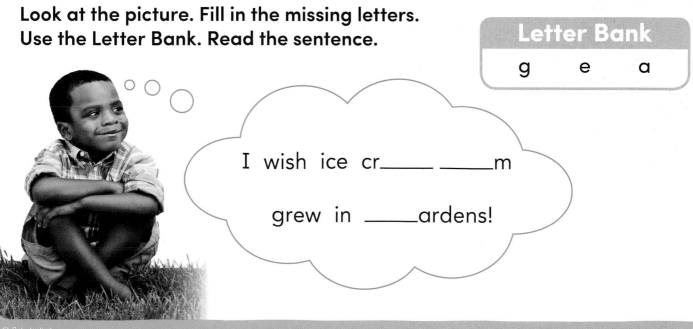

I wish ice cr_____ _____m

grew in _____ardens!

How Long Is It?

How many erasers long is each item? Write the answer.

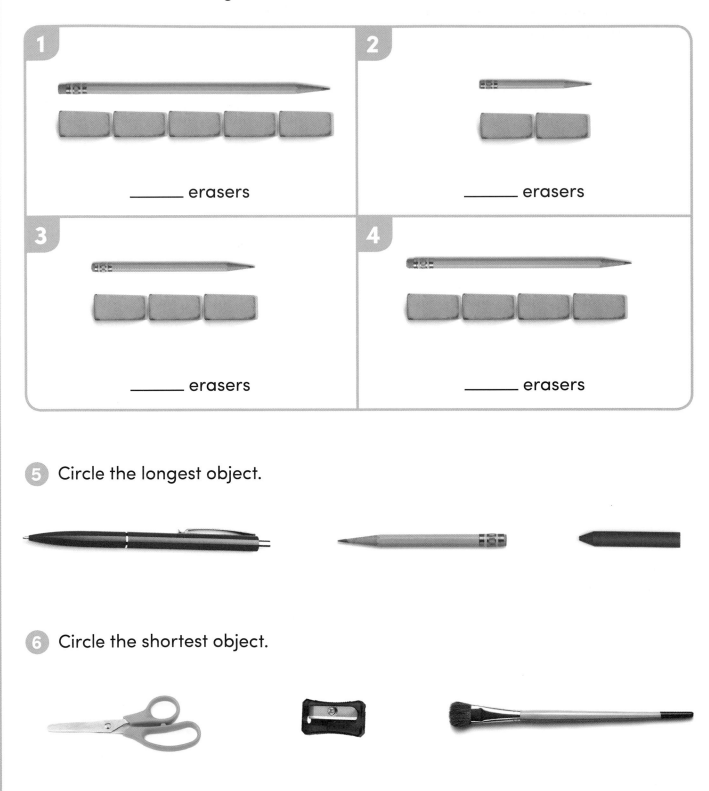

1

_____ erasers

2

_____ erasers

3

_____ erasers

4

_____ erasers

5 Circle the longest object.

6 Circle the shortest object.

Four Seasons on a Farm

What happens throughout the year on a farm?
Look at each picture. Circle the word for each picture, then write it.
Use the words to tell a story about a farm.

hoe   hop

_____

boat   grow

_____

mow   more

_____

saw   snow

_____

Look at the picture fill in the missing letters.
Use the Letter Bank. Read the sentence.

Letter Bank
a   o

A baby horse is a f _____ _____l.

What Time Is It?

Look at the clocks below. Write the time each clock shows.

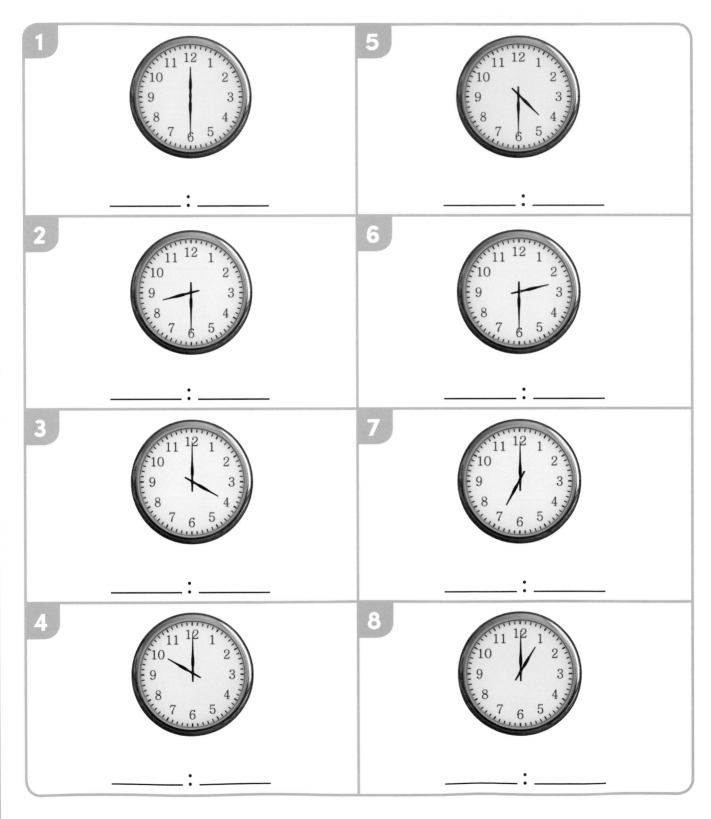

1. _____ : _____

5. _____ : _____

2. _____ : _____

6. _____ : _____

3. _____ : _____

7. _____ : _____

4. _____ : _____

8. _____ : _____

It's Raining

Look at the Word Bank.
Use the words to fill in the blanks.
Then read the story.

Word Bank

looked   picked   started   flying   playing

Leo and I were _____ a game outside.

Then it _____ to rain.

We _____ up our game and ran inside.

Then we _____ out the window.

Birds were _____ to their nests.

They wanted to stay dry, too!

Find and circle the Word Bank words in the word search.

p	l	a	y	i	n	g	l
i	y	j	z	b	r	e	o
c	f	l	y	i	n	g	o
k	m	x	r	q	x	w	k
e	j	g	s	k	p	z	e
d	s	t	a	r	t	e	d

75

Greater Than, Less Than, or Equal To?

Compare the numbers using >, <, or =.

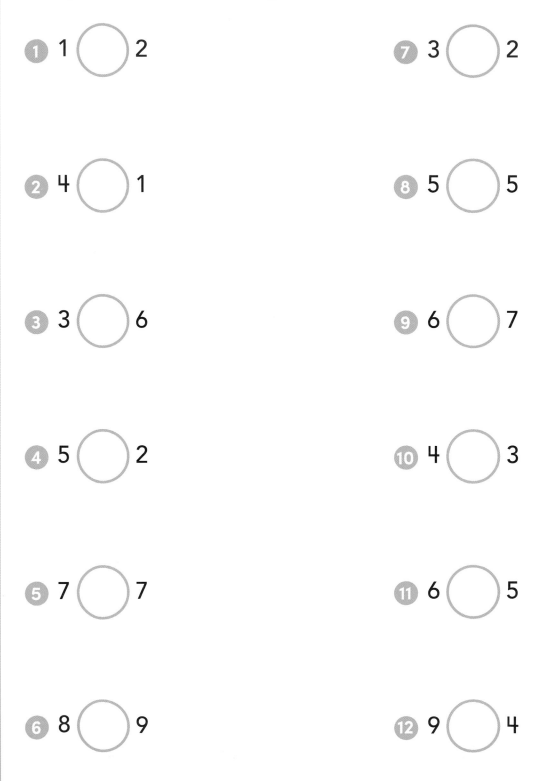

1 1 ◯ 2

2 4 ◯ 1

3 3 ◯ 6

4 5 ◯ 2

5 7 ◯ 7

6 8 ◯ 9

7 3 ◯ 2

8 5 ◯ 5

9 6 ◯ 7

10 4 ◯ 3

11 6 ◯ 5

12 9 ◯ 4

Positional Words

Draw lines to connect each sentence to its picture.

Word Bank

| on | off | over | under | before | after | up | down | around | into |

1 The girl goes **up** the ladder.

2 The girl goes **down** the slide.

3 The dog is **under** the stool.

4 The cat jumps **off** the chair.

5 The cat is **on** the bed.

6 The cat jumps **over** the water.

7 The cat jumped **into** his arms.

8 The cat goes **around** the box.

9 The cat jumps **before** the dog.

10 The boy will put on his shoes **after** his socks.

What's at the Store?

It's time to add up items at the toy store. Read each problem.
Then write an equation to answer the question.

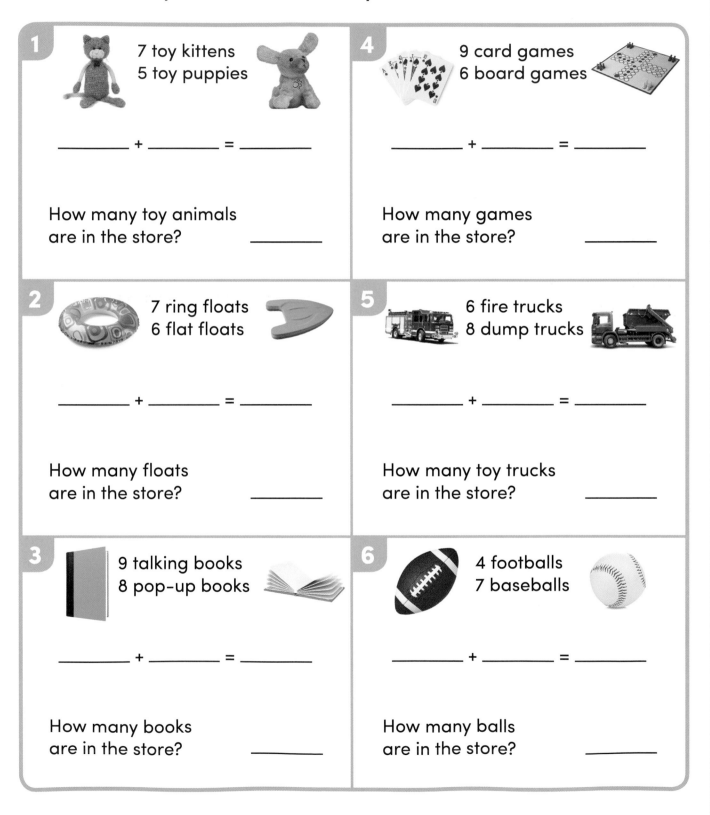

1

7 toy kittens
5 toy puppies

_____ + _____ = _____

How many toy animals
are in the store?   _____

2

7 ring floats
6 flat floats

_____ + _____ = _____

How many floats
are in the store?   _____

3

9 talking books
8 pop-up books

_____ + _____ = _____

How many books
are in the store?   _____

4

9 card games
6 board games

_____ + _____ = _____

How many games
are in the store?   _____

5

6 fire trucks
8 dump trucks

_____ + _____ = _____

How many toy trucks
are in the store?   _____

6

4 footballs
7 baseballs

_____ + _____ = _____

How many balls
are in the store?   _____

A Dolphin Boat

Read the article. Then answer the questions.

Most boats glide on top of the water. This boat does not. It moves like a dolphin!

The boat has fins and a tail. They help the boat change direction like a real dolphin's fin and tail do. The boat can dive under the water. Then it can jump 10 feet into the air.

Two people can fit inside the boat.

1. The **title** is at the top of an article. It is big. It can tell what the article is about. Circle the title.

2. A **caption** is on or near a picture. It tells about a picture. Underline the caption.

3. What is this article mostly about?
   - ○ a dolphin boat
   - ○ a dolphin tail
   - ○ the water

4. What do the dolphin boat and real dolphins both have?
   - ○ a heart
   - ○ fins and a tail
   - ○ a wheel

Missing Sums

Find the missing number in the equation. Use the commutative property.

1. $6 + 8 = 14$

   $8 + 6 =$ _____

2. $4 + 3 = 7$

   $3 +$ _____ $= 7$

3. $5 + 4 = 9$

   $4 + 5 =$ _____

4. $9 + 8 = 17$

   _____ $+ 9 = 17$

5. $9 + 5 = 14$

   $5 +$ _____ $= 14$

6. $9 + 2 = 11$

   _____ $+ 9 = 11$

7. $9 + 7 = 16$

   $7 + 9 =$ _____

8. $7 + 5 = 12$

   _____ $+ 7 = 12$

9. $1 + 9 = 10$

   $9 +$ _____ $= 10$

10. $10 + 6 = 16$

    $6 + 10 =$ _____

Help Your Child Get Ready: Week 7

Here are some activities that you and your child might enjoy.

Who Is It?

Play a guessing game. Give your child clues about someone your family knows. Can he or she guess this person's identity? Trade roles. Play again.

What's My Sign?

When you go places with your child, ask him or her to look around and record as many signs and symbols as possible and then share the list. Discuss why some road signs do not have words and others do. Encourage your child to make up his or her own "road signs" to post around your home.

Two-Minute Lists

Give your child two minutes to list as many plural words as he or she can think of that end with the letter *s*.

Summer Games

Plan a mini "Summer Olympics" with your family. Play classic picnic games such as a water-balloon toss or a three-legged race, or make up fun games of your own. Take turns trying them!

These are the skills your child will be working on this week.

Math
- addition and subtraction within 18
- use a number line to subtract

Reading
- retell key details

Phonics & Vocabulary
- long vowels
- ending digraph: *ck*
- compound words

Grammar & Writing
- use commas in a series
- use adjectives

Incentive Chart: Week 7

Week 7	Day 1	Day 2	Day 3	Day 4	Day 5
Put a sticker to show you completed each day's work.	☆ ☆	☆ ☆	☆ ☆	☆ ☆	☆ ☆

CONGRATULATIONS!

Wow! You did a great job this week!

This certificate is presented to:

_____

_____   _____
Date   Parent/Caregiver's Signature

A Tight Squeeze

The long-vowel sounds can be spelled with the following letters:

long *a*:	long *e*:	long *i*:	long *o*:
a_e, ay, ai	ee, e_e	i_e	o_e

Read the words in the Word Bank. Underline the letters that make the long-vowel sound in each word. Use the words to complete the lists below.

Word Bank

cake	nail	tray	seed
nine	nose	kite	here

Words with long-*a* sound	Words with long-*e* sound	Words with long-*i* sound	Words with long-*o* sound
_____	_____	_____	_____
_____	_____	_____	_____
_____	_____	_____	_____

Write the word from the Word Bank that belongs with each group below.

1 _____

2 _____

3 _____

4 _____

5 _____

6 _____

Race Through the Facts

Add or subtract.
The race car that ends with the highest number wins the race!

© Scholastic Inc.

Commas in a Series

Some sentences include a list. A **comma** (,) is used to separate each item in the list.

For example: *Mrs. Jones asked the class to work on pages two, three, and four.*

Fill in the blanks to make a list in each sentence.
Watch for commas!

1 The birds built their nests using

_____, _____,

and _____.

2 I ate _____, _____,

and _____ for breakfast.

3 We stayed with Grandma on _____,

_____, and _____ nights.

4 I found _____, _____,

and _____ in my party bag.

5 The boys played _____, _____,

and _____ at summer camp.

6 The _____, _____,

and _____ ate the corn we scattered.

Using a Number Line

Find the difference. Use the number line to help you.

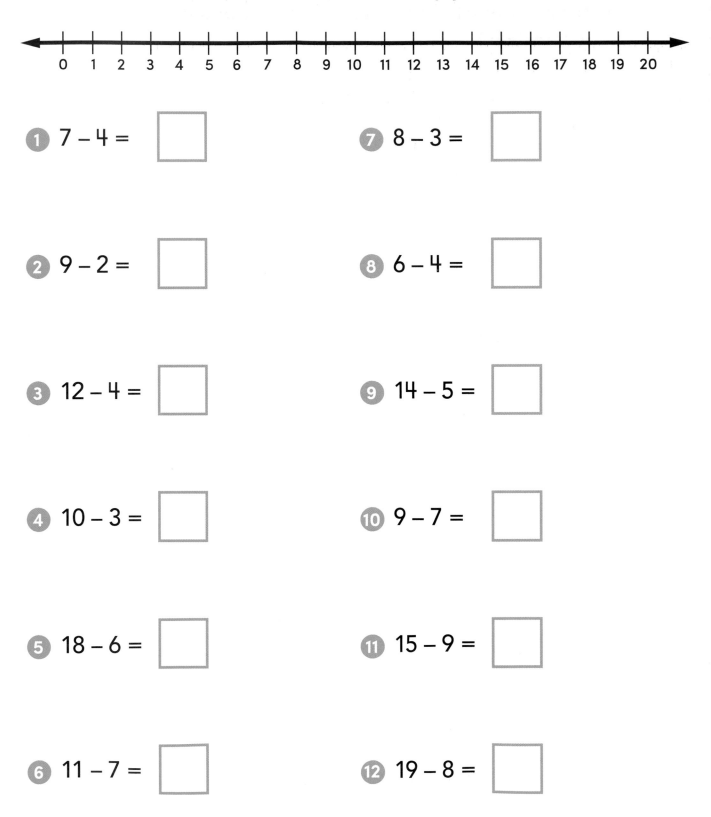

1. 7 – 4 = ☐

2. 9 – 2 = ☐

3. 12 – 4 = ☐

4. 10 – 3 = ☐

5. 18 – 6 = ☐

6. 11 – 7 = ☐

7. 8 – 3 = ☐

8. 6 – 4 = ☐

9. 14 – 5 = ☐

10. 9 – 7 = ☐

11. 15 – 9 = ☐

12. 19 – 8 = ☐

Describing Words

Read each sentence. Trace the word. Next to each picture, write the number of the sentence that describes it. Read each sentence again. The first one is done for you.

1. A toothpick is thin. thin

2. A telephone pole is thick. thick

3. An ice skating rink is smooth. smooth

4. A rocky path is bumpy. bumpy

5. A teddy bear is fuzzy. fuzzy

6. A kitten is soft. soft

7. A sidewalk is hard. hard

8. A chick is fluffy. fluffy

9. A new coin is shiny. shiny

10. Honey is sticky. sticky

Describing Words

Write the best word to complete each sentence.

1 Cotton candy is _____.

2 Before it is cooked, a potato is _____.

3 A peach's skin is _____.

4 A needle is _____.

5 Mashed potatoes are _____.

Word Bank

thin	fuzzy
soft	hard
fluffy	

Look at the words in the Word Bank.
Find and circle each word in the word search.

c	t	i	s	n	r	a
s	h	i	n	y	b	h
m	s	j	o	w	u	v
o	s	h	y	b	m	l
o	w	j	q	b	p	i
t	h	i	c	k	y	a
h	s	t	i	c	k	y

Word Bank

thick	smooth
bumpy	shiny
sticky	

Check it Out!

The letters **ck** make the sound at the end of the word *pick*.

Read the words in the Word Bank. Circle the letters ck in each word. Use the words to complete the lists below.

Word Bank

duck	pack	stick	back
neck	rock	clock	quick

Words with short-*a* sound	Words with short-*e* sound	Words with short-*o* sound
_____	_____	_____
_____	_____	_____

Words with short-*i* sound	Words with short-*u* sound
_____	_____
_____	_____

Write the word from the Word Bank that best matches each picture.

1 _____

2 _____

3 _____

4 _____

Break the Code

Subtract.

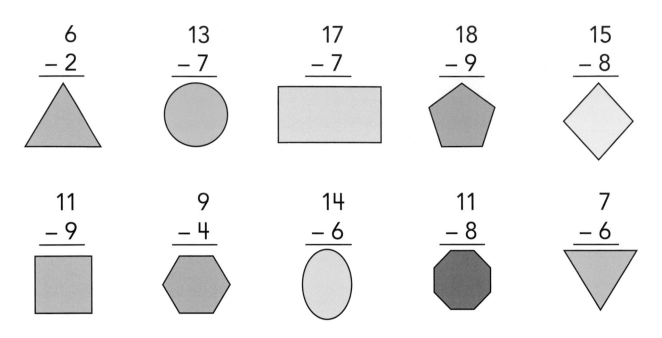

$$\begin{array}{r} 6 \\ -2 \\ \hline \end{array}$$ △

$$\begin{array}{r} 13 \\ -7 \\ \hline \end{array}$$ ◯

$$\begin{array}{r} 17 \\ -7 \\ \hline \end{array}$$ ▭

$$\begin{array}{r} 18 \\ -9 \\ \hline \end{array}$$ ⬠

$$\begin{array}{r} 15 \\ -8 \\ \hline \end{array}$$ ◆

$$\begin{array}{r} 11 \\ -9 \\ \hline \end{array}$$ ▢

$$\begin{array}{r} 9 \\ -4 \\ \hline \end{array}$$ ⬡

$$\begin{array}{r} 14 \\ -6 \\ \hline \end{array}$$ ⬭

$$\begin{array}{r} 11 \\ -8 \\ \hline \end{array}$$ ⯃

$$\begin{array}{r} 7 \\ -6 \\ \hline \end{array}$$ ▽

Use the answers above to solve each problem.

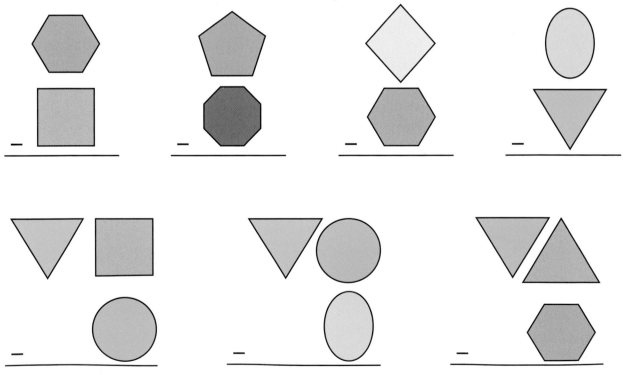

Going to Granny's

Read the story. Then answer the questions.

Kelly is going to spend the night with her grandmother. She will need to take her pajamas, a T-shirt, and some shorts. Into the suitcase go her toothbrush, toothpaste, and hairbrush. Granny told her to bring a swimsuit in case it was warm enough to swim. Mom said to pack her favorite pillow and storybook. Dad said, "Don't forget to take Granny's sunglasses that she left here last week." Now Kelly is ready to go!

1 Circle the things that Kelly packed in her suitcase.

2 A **compound word** is a word that is made up of two smaller words. For example, *cow + boy = cowboy*. Find and circle eight compound words in the story.

A Nutty Bunch

Add or subtract. Circle the nut if the answer matches the squirrel.

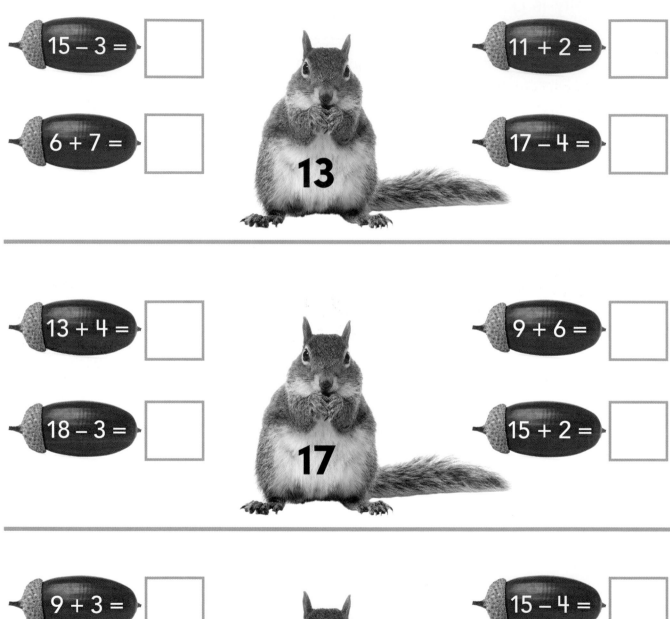

$15 - 3 =$ ☐

$6 + 7 =$ ☐

$11 + 2 =$ ☐

$17 - 4 =$ ☐

13

$13 + 4 =$ ☐

$18 - 3 =$ ☐

$9 + 6 =$ ☐

$15 + 2 =$ ☐

17

$9 + 3 =$ ☐

$8 + 3 =$ ☐

$15 - 4 =$ ☐

$18 - 7 =$ ☐

11

Help Your Child Get Ready: Week 8

Here are some activities that you and your child might enjoy.

Less Is More

Provide your child with a reclosable bag containing 25 pennies, 5 nickels, and 1 quarter. Encourage him or her to count the pennies by arranging them into groups of 5. Explain that a quarter is worth 25 cents and 5 nickels also equals 25 cents. Ask questions such as: *How many pennies are in a nickel? Which is worth more: 75 pennies or 4 quarters?*

Simon Says

This favorite game can be used to practice a specific skill or concept such as prepositions. For example, say, *"Simon says, Put your hands behind your back,"* or, *"Simon says, Walk across the room,"* or *"Simon says, Put your palm under your chin."* Remind your child to follow instructions only when "Simon Says."

Sidewalk Chalkboard

Your child may find practicing spelling words or handwriting more like play when using colorful sidewalk chalk outdoors. Challenge your child to write words as big as possible, then as small as possible.

Surprise Story

Cut out ten pictures from a magazine. Put them in a bag. Invite your child to take them out one at a time to tell a story.

These are the skills your child will be working on this week.

Math
- identify attributes of a shape
- addition and subtraction within 100
- subtract multiples of 10
- make shapes
- skip count by 10s
- solve word problems

Reading
- sort and classify words
- compare and contrast
- identify the main idea

Phonics & Vocabulary
- synonyms

Grammar & Writing
- use adjectives

Incentive Chart: Week 8

Week 8	Day 1	Day 2	Day 3	Day 4	Day 5
Put a sticker to show you completed each day's work.	☆ ☆	☆ ☆	☆ ☆	☆ ☆	☆ ☆

CONGRATULATIONS!

Wow! You did a great job this week!

This certificate is presented to:

_____

_____   _____
Date   Parent/Caregiver's Signature

More Describing Words

How would you describe a lollipop or a baby chick? Complete the chart below with describing words for each. Choose words from the Word Bank.

Word Bank

thin	thick	smooth	bumpy	fuzzy
soft	hard	fluffy	shiny	sticky

Lollipop

Chick

_____   _____

_____   _____

_____   _____

_____   _____

1 Name something that is thin. _____

2 Name something that is thick. _____

3 Name something that is bumpy. _____

Just Geometry

Put on your thinking cap to solve these problems.

1 How many sides are on each shape?

   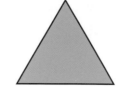   

_____ sides   _____ sides   _____ sides

2 Circle the name of each shape.

   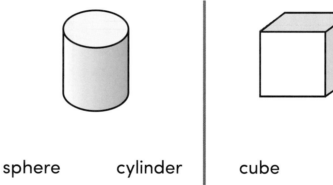

cone   cube | sphere   cylinder | cube   sphere

3 Find each shape sum. Use the numbers in the shapes below.

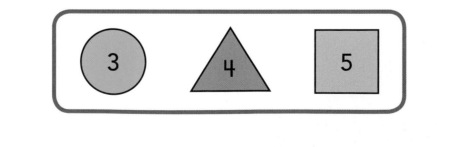

= _____   = _____

Going to the Mall

Read the words in the Word Bank. Write each word in the place where you would find these items at the mall.

Word Bank

tickets	sandals	tacos	beans	big screen
tulip bulb	peppers	fertilizer	popcorn	soil
sneakers	burritos	boots	pots	candy

Sadie's Shoe Store

_____

_____

_____

_____

MOVIE TOWN CINEMA

_____

_____

_____

_____

Pepe's Mexican Food

_____

_____

_____

GARDEN SHOP

_____

_____

_____

_____

Opposites Attract

Add or subtract. Draw a line to connect the magnets with the same answer. Read the words in each connecting set of magnets.

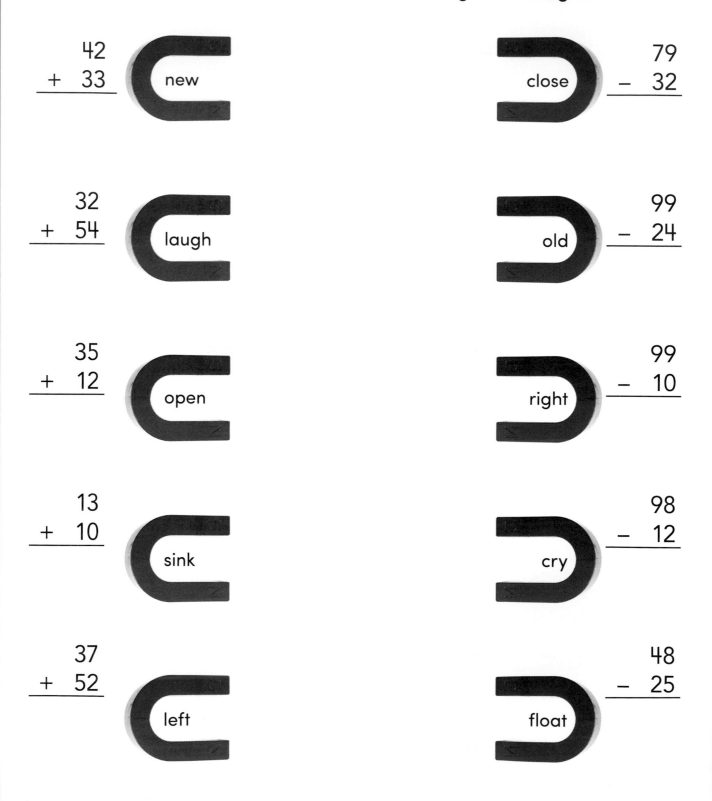

42
+ 33
new

79
close − 32

32
+ 54
laugh

99
old − 24

35
+ 12
open

99
right − 10

13
+ 10
sink

98
cry − 12

37
+ 52
left

48
float − 25

Same But Different

Circle the word that is almost the same as the first word.

	seat	like	horse	chair
	down	egg	below	shell
	sleep	rest	drive	fun
	jump	third	hop	good
	road	street	bike	car
	lake	fall	back	pond
	mix	spoon	stir	pen
	plate	find	dish	grow

Multiples of 10

Find the difference. Use the hundreds chart to help you.

1	2	3	4	5	6	7	8	9	10
11	12	13	14	15	16	17	18	19	20
21	22	23	24	25	26	27	28	29	30
31	32	33	34	35	36	37	38	39	40
41	42	43	44	45	46	47	48	49	50
51	52	53	54	55	56	57	58	59	60
61	62	63	64	65	66	67	68	69	70
71	72	73	74	75	76	77	78	79	80
81	82	83	84	85	86	87	88	89	90
91	92	93	94	95	96	97	98	99	100

1 50 – 10 = _____

2 70 – 10 = _____

3 80 – 30 = _____

4 70 – 60 = _____

5 80 – 60 = _____

6 60 – 10 = _____

7 20 – 10 = _____

8 50 – 20 = _____

9 90 – 20 = _____

10 40 – 30 = _____

11 70 – 40 = _____

12 90 – 30 = _____

Moles, Voles, or Both?

Read. Then answer the questions.

Moles and Voles

Moles and voles are both found in North America. They are alike in many ways. They are also different. Both moles and voles are small animals. Both cause problems for gardeners. Moles and voles both dig a lot. This hurts gardens. Read below how moles and voles are different.

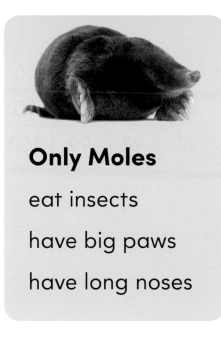

Only Moles

eat insects

have big paws

have long noses

Only Voles

eat plants

have small paws

have short noses

1 What can both animals hurt?

_____

2 Which animal eats plants?

_____

3 Which animal has big paws?

_____

Making Shapes

Some shapes are shown below. They have extra shapes next to them.
Make a new shape by tracing the extra shapes. Then color in the shapes.

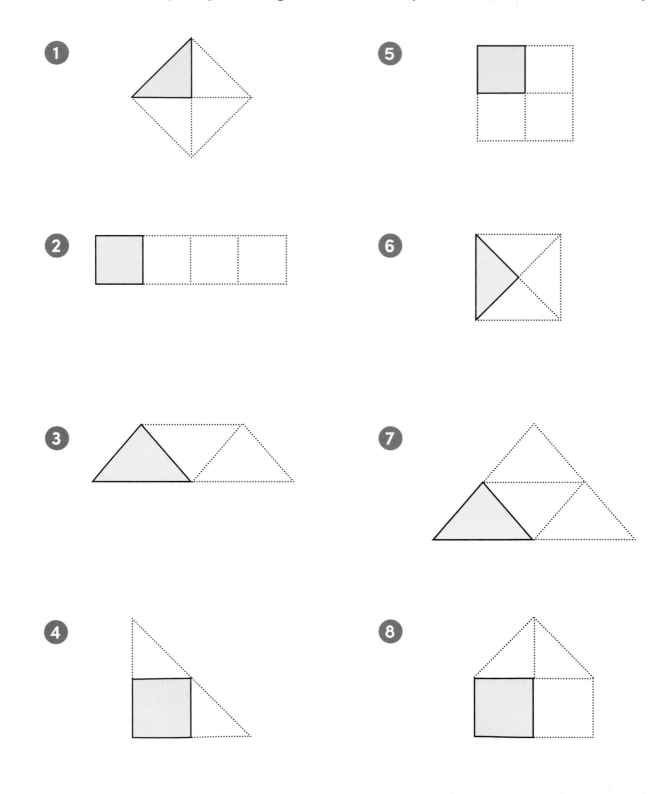

Trucks

Read about trucks. Then follow the directions below.

Trucks do important work. Dump trucks carry away sand and rocks. Cement trucks have a barrel that turns round and round. They deliver cement to workers who are making sidewalks. Fire trucks carry water hoses and firefighters. Gasoline is delivered in large tank trucks. Flat bed trucks carry wood to people who are building houses.

1 What is the main idea of the paragraph? Write it in the circle below.

2 Draw a line from the main idea to the trucks described in the paragraph.

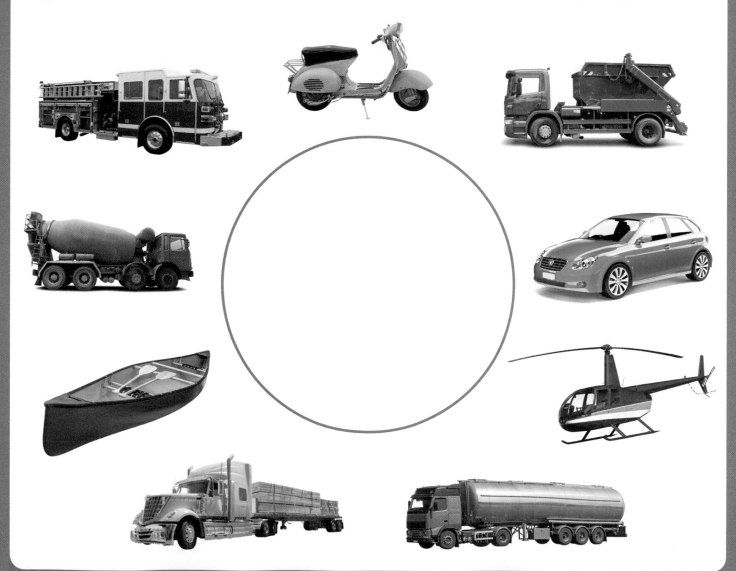

Mixed Math

Skip count aloud by 10s. Write each number you say.

10, _____, _____, _____, _____,

_____, _____, _____, _____, 100

Fast Practice
Add.

44	38	51	62	17	29
+ 30	+ 50	+ 40	+ 20	+ 60	+ 70
☐	☐	☐	☐	☐	☐

Solve It!

Each house on Key Road has a number. The first five house numbers are 101, 103, 105, 107, and 109. What is the next number?

Show your work.

The next number is _____.

Help Your Child Get Ready: Week 9

Here are some activities that you and your child might enjoy.

Give Me a Foot!

Cut two 12-inch-long pieces of yarn or string. Give the yarn to your child and ask him or her to find something shorter than 12 inches and one thing longer than 12 inches. Can your child find something that is exactly 12 inches? Challenge your child to find something that is 24 inches!

Summer Fun

Give your child a sheet of paper. Ask your child to list things he or she loves about summer. Your child has made a list poem! Encourage your child to give it a title and read it aloud to the family.

ABC Order

Read a list of five to seven words to your child, such as the days of the week or the ingredients for a tasty sandwich. Then have him or her put the words in alphabetical order.

Listen and Draw

Describe an object, animal, or person to your child. Ask him or her to draw it. How close does the drawing come to looking like the real thing? Then ask him or her to describe something for you to draw.

These are the skills your child will be working on this week.

Math

- add multiples of 10
- tell time
- addition within 20
- use a graph to represent data
- identify patterns
- skip count backwards by 10s
- subtract 2-digit numbers
- solve word problems

Reading

- sequence
- analyze characters

Phonics & Vocabulary

- consonants
- vowels
- sort and classify words

Grammar & Writing

- capitalization
- punctuation

Incentive Chart: Week 9

Week 9	Day 1	Day 2	Day 3	Day 4	Day 5
Put a sticker to show you completed each day's work.	☆ ☆	☆ ☆	☆ ☆	☆ ☆	☆ ☆

CONGRATULATIONS!

Wow! You did a great job this week!

This certificate is presented to:

_____

_____   _____
Date   Parent/Caregiver's Signature

Find the Missing Letter

Consonants

Look at each picture. Write the missing letter to complete the word.

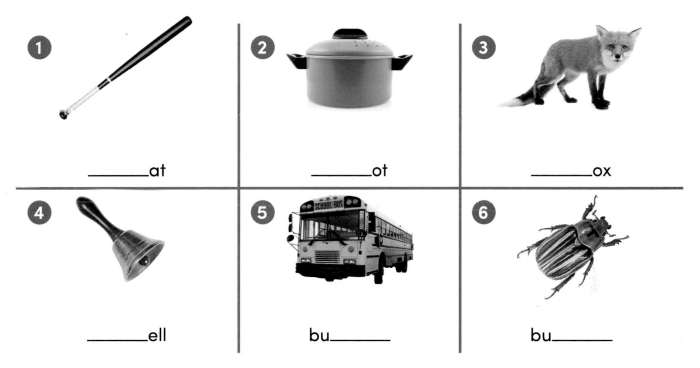

1 _____at

2 _____ot

3 _____ox

4 _____ell

5 bu_____

6 bu_____

Vowels

Look at each picture. Write the missing letter to complete the word.

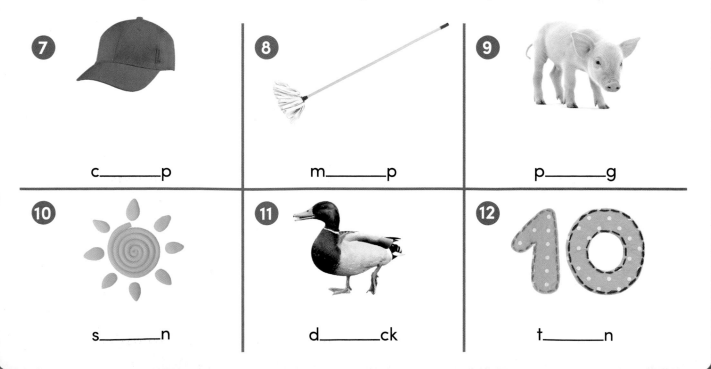

7 c____p

8 m____p

9 p____g

10 s____n

11 d____ck

12 t____n

Add Multiples of 10

What number is 10 more? Use the hundreds chart to help you.

1 72 + 10 = _____

2 28 + 10 = _____

3 54 + 10 = _____

4 32 + 10 = _____

1	2	3	4	5	6	7	8	9	10
11	12	13	14	15	16	17	18	19	20
21	22	23	24	25	26	27	28	29	30
31	32	33	34	35	36	37	38	39	40
41	42	43	44	45	46	47	48	49	50
51	52	53	54	55	56	57	58	59	60
61	62	63	64	65	66	67	68	69	70
71	72	73	74	75	76	77	78	79	80
81	82	83	84	85	86	87	88	89	90
91	92	93	94	95	96	97	98	99	100

What is the sum? Use the hundreds chart to help you.

5 26 + 50 = _____

6 38 + 30 = _____

7 17 + 60 = _____

8 42 + 40 = _____

1	2	3	4	5	6	7	8	9	10
11	12	13	14	15	16	17	18	19	20
21	22	23	24	25	26	27	28	29	30
31	32	33	34	35	36	37	38	39	40
41	42	43	44	45	46	47	48	49	50
51	52	53	54	55	56	57	58	59	60
61	62	63	64	65	66	67	68	69	70
71	72	73	74	75	76	77	78	79	80
81	82	83	84	85	86	87	88	89	90
91	92	93	94	95	96	97	98	99	100

A Happy Camper

Complete each sentence below.

1 Every sentence begins with a _____ .

2 A statement ends with a _____ .

3 A question ends with a _____ .

Read Dalton's letter. It looks like he was in a hurry when he wrote it. Help him find ten mistakes. Circle them.

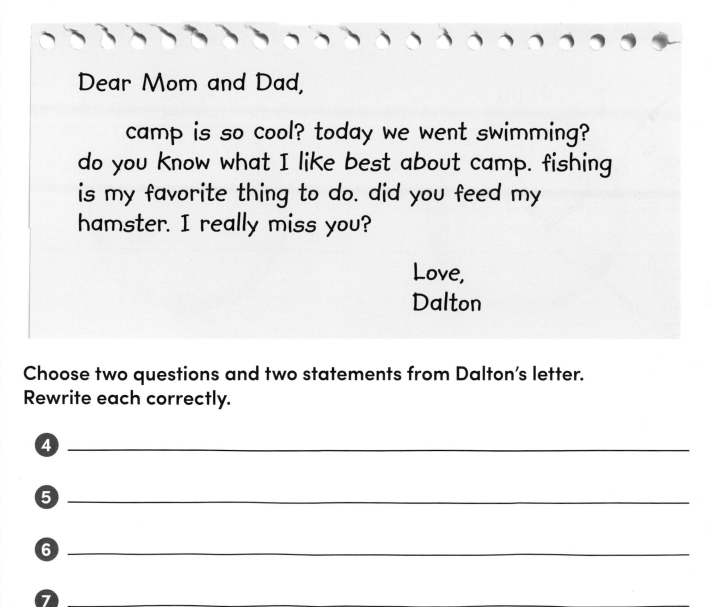

Dear Mom and Dad,

   camp is so cool? today we went swimming? do you know what I like best about camp. fishing is my favorite thing to do. did you feed my hamster. I really miss you?

                    Love,
                    Dalton

Choose two questions and two statements from Dalton's letter. Rewrite each correctly.

4 _____

5 _____

6 _____

7 _____

Tick-Tock Clocks

Draw hands to show each time.

2:00

6:00

11:00

10:30

5:30

9:00

Going Swimming

Read the story.

Tomorrow I will go swimming. I will put on my swimsuit. I will jump in the water to get wet. Then I will dive off the diving board. Grandma will fix lunch for me. Mom will swim with me after lunch.

**Read the sentences below.
Rewrite them in the correct order.**

Mom will swim with me after lunch.

I will put on my swimsuit.

Grandma will fix lunch for me.

I will jump in the water.

1 _____

_____

2 _____

_____

3 _____

_____

4 _____

_____

Ocean Math

Circle the two numbers that make 10.
Then add. The first one is done for you.
Solve the riddle using your answers.

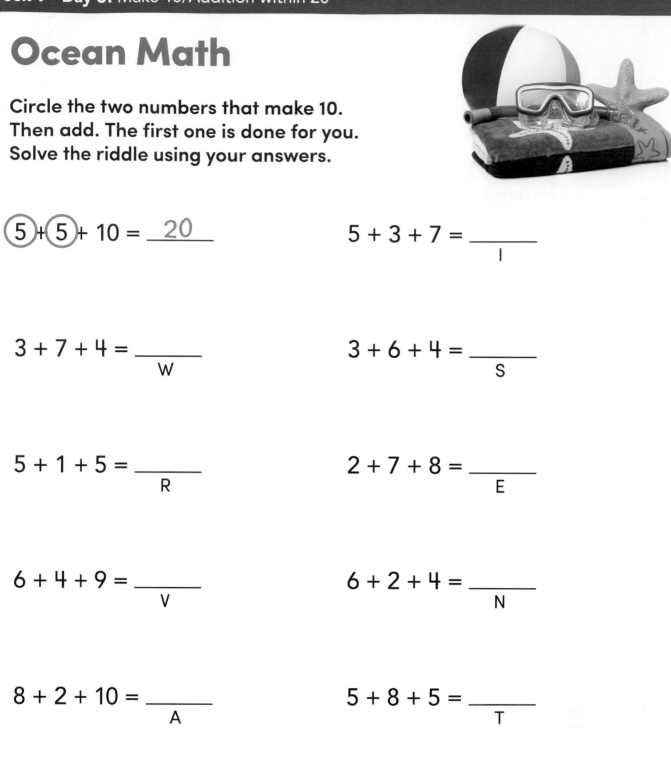

(5) + (5) + 10 = __20__

5 + 3 + 7 = _____
                 I

3 + 7 + 4 = _____
                 W

3 + 6 + 4 = _____
                 S

5 + 1 + 5 = _____
                 R

2 + 7 + 8 = _____
                 E

6 + 4 + 9 = _____
                 V

6 + 2 + 4 = _____
                 N

8 + 2 + 10 = _____
                  A

5 + 8 + 5 = _____
                 T

Write the letter that goes with each number.

What does the ocean do when it sees the beach?

___ ___   ___ ___ ___ ___ ___ .
15   18   14   20   19   17   13

Family Word Sort

Sort the words from the Word Bank. Then write them in the correct boxes.

Word Bank

mother	father	sister	brother	daughter
son	baby	grandma	grandpa	

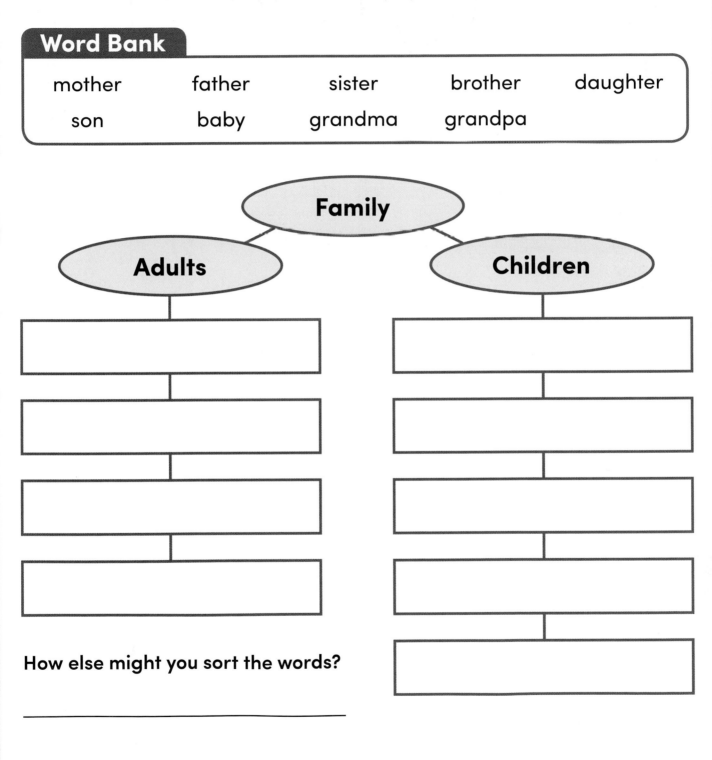

Family

Adults

Children

How else might you sort the words?

_____

_____

_____

Animal Chart

Count each kind of animal. Show how many in the graph.
Color one box for each animal you count.

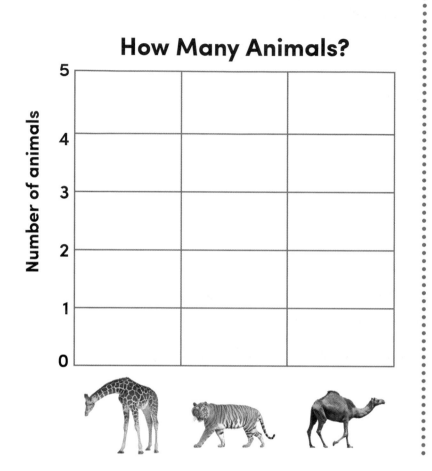

How Many Animals?

Write the numbers to complete each pattern.

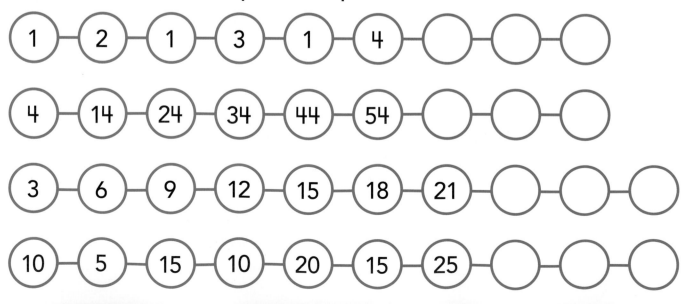

1 — 2 — 1 — 3 — 1 — 4 — ◯ — ◯ — ◯

4 — 14 — 24 — 34 — 44 — 54 — ◯ — ◯ — ◯

3 — 6 — 9 — 12 — 15 — 18 — 21 — ◯ — ◯ — ◯

10 — 5 — 15 — 10 — 20 — 15 — 25 — ◯ — ◯ — ◯

The New House

Read the story. Then answer the questions.

Glen's parents bought a new house. The new house is bigger than the house they live in now. It has a huge back yard, too. His parents are fixing it up. It's not done yet. Glen and his family will move as soon as it is finished. They hope to move before school starts.

Today, Glen saw his new house. He loves his new room. He will share the room with his brother Jim. The room is big and sunny. It will have bunk beds. Glen hopes he gets to sleep on top. At first Glen was unsure about moving. Now, he's excited. He'll make lots of new friends. He's also not moving very far. He'll still be able to see all of his old friends.

1 What does Glen like about the new house?

_____

_____

2 How does Glen feel about moving after seeing the house?
- ○ excited
- ○ scared
- ○ unsure

3 Who will Glen share his new room with?
- ○ no one
- ○ his friend Jim
- ○ his brother Jim

Mixed Math

Count back aloud by 10s. Write each number you say.

100, _____, _____, _____, _____,

_____, _____, _____, _____, 10, 0

Fast Practice
Subtract.

$$
\begin{array}{r} 85 \\ -\ 60 \\ \hline \end{array}
\qquad
\begin{array}{r} 92 \\ -\ 70 \\ \hline \end{array}
\qquad
\begin{array}{r} 51 \\ -\ 40 \\ \hline \end{array}
\qquad
\begin{array}{r} 64 \\ -\ 30 \\ \hline \end{array}
\qquad
\begin{array}{r} 78 \\ -\ 50 \\ \hline \end{array}
\qquad
\begin{array}{r} 39 \\ -\ 20 \\ \hline \end{array}
$$

Solve It!

The art teacher gets 32 new paintbrushes and 45 new markers. How many new art items is this in all?

Show your work.

There are _____ new art items.

Help Your Child Get Ready: Week 10

Here are some activities that you and your child might enjoy.

Time for Review

With your child, find out the time for sunrise and sunset, and determine the current time of day. Ask questions such as: *What time will it be in one hour? What time was it one hour ago? What time will it be in 15 minutes? How many hours are there between sunrise and sunset? How many hours are there between sunset and sunrise?*

Imagine That!

Invite your child to close his or her eyes. Then ask, *What sounds do you hear?* See if your child can name ten.

Mum's the Word

This is a fun dinnertime family game. Agree on a small word that is used frequently in conversation, such as *the* or *and*. This word becomes "mum." No one can say it! Anyone who does, drops out. The last person left is the winner.

Comic Mix-Up

Build up your child's sequencing skills. Cut a comic strip into sections. Ask your child to put the strip in the correct order and to explain his or her thinking.

These are the skills your child will be working on this week.

Math

- make shapes
- identify a number that is 10 less
- tell time
- solve word problems
- identify attributes of a shape
- compare numbers
- place value
- add doubles

Reading

- analyze characters
- identify key details

Phonics & Vocabulary

- beginning and ending consonants
- spelling

Incentive Chart: Week 10

Week 10	Day 1	Day 2	Day 3	Day 4	Day 5
Put a sticker to show you completed each day's work.	☆ ☆	☆ ☆	☆ ☆	☆ ☆	☆ ☆

CONGRATULATIONS!

Wow! You did a great job this week!

This certificate is presented to:

_____

_____   _____
Date   Parent/Caregiver's Signature

Fill-In Story

Look at the pictures. Fill in the missing letters. Use the Letter Bank. Then read the story.

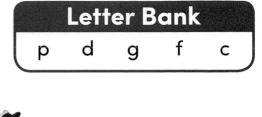

"Moo, moo," says the _____ow.

"Baa, baa," says the shee____.

"Oink, oink," says the pi_____.

"Quack, quack," says the _____uck.

What a noisy _____arm!

Say the name for each picture. Fill in the missing letter. Use the Letter Bank.

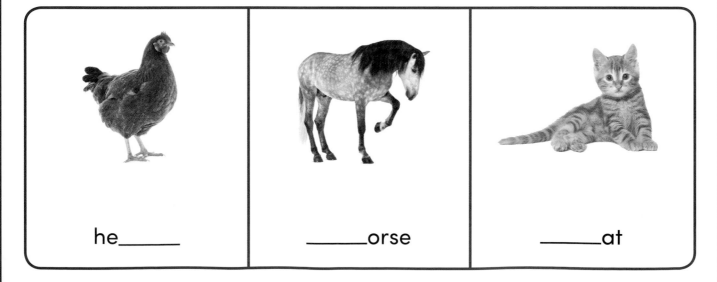

| he_____ | _____orse | _____at |

Shaping Up

Draw the shape shown in each box. Then color each shape.

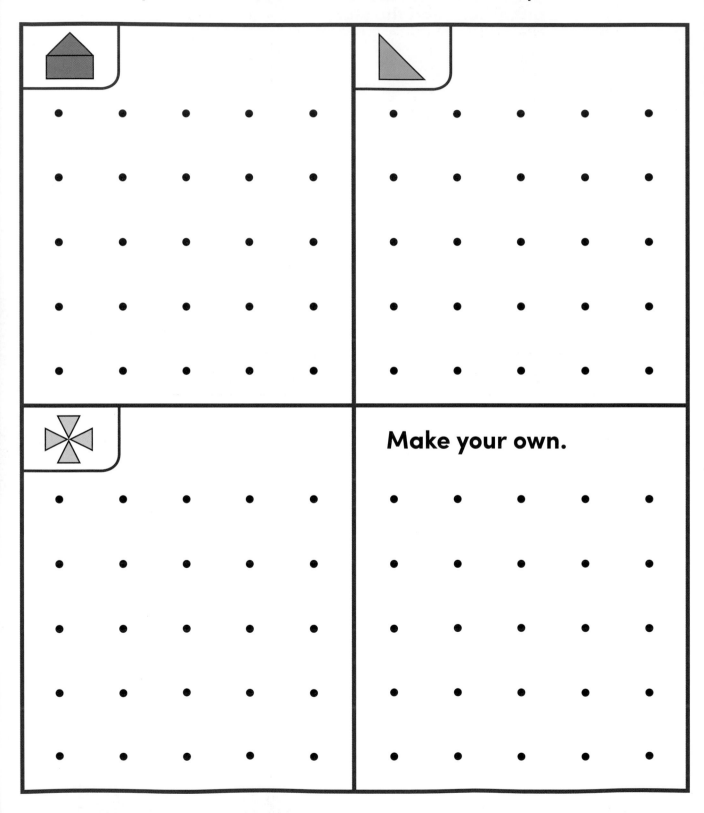

Make your own.

Two-Way Words

Use the Letter Banks and pictures to complete each activity.

1 Fill in the missing letters to make two words.

Letter Bank

f	m	s	t

2 Fill in the missing letters. Read the word.

Letter Bank

d	s

_____pi_____er

3 Read each word below. Change one letter to make a new word. Read the new word.

Letter Bank

r	t

fun

_____un

cap

ca_____

Mixed Math

Write the number that is 10 less.

13 _____   74 _____   98 _____

61 _____   85 _____   72 _____

Fast Practice

Draw hands to show each time.

2:00   6:00   11:00

Solve It!

A zoo has 14 monkeys and 11 parrots. Each gets 1 apple a day. How many apples do all the animals eat in 2 days?

Show your work.

They eat _____ apples in all.

A Trip to the Movies

Use the price list to answer the questions.

Prices

Child's Ticket $8

Large Popcorn $5

Small Popcorn $4

Large Soda $3

Small Soda. $2

Renee has $20. She goes to the movies.

1 How much money does Renee have after she buys a ticket? _____

2 Her dad told her to bring home $5. But Renee wants popcorn and soda.

What can she order?_____

_____

3 How much would it cost for 4 children to buy movie tickets?_____

Corners and Sides

How many corners are in each shape?

1

_____ corners

2

_____ corners

3

_____ corners

4

_____ corners

5

_____ corners

6

_____ corners

How many sides are in each shape?

7 square _____

8 triangle _____

9 rectangle _____

10 pentagon _____

Draw three different shapes, each with four corners and four sides.

Mixed-Up Margie

A **character** is a person or animal in a story. To help readers understand a character better, a story often gives details about the character.

Once upon a time there was a mixed-up queen named Margie. She got things mixed up. She wore her crown on her arm. She wore a shoe on her head. She painted every fingernail a different color. Then she painted her nose red! She used a fork to hold her hair in place. She wore a purple belt around her knees. The king didn't mind. He alway wore his clothes backward!

Use the story and your crayons to help you follow these instructions:

1 Draw Margie a crown.

2 Draw her shoe.

3 Paint her fingernails and nose.

4 Draw what goes in her hair.

5 Draw her belt.

Fill in the bubble next to the correct answer.

6 What makes you think Margie is mixed up?
   ○ the way she dresses
   ○ the way she talks

7 What makes you think the king is mixed up, too?
   ○ He talks backward.
   ○ He wears his clothes backward.

Compare Numbers

Compare the numbers. Use >, <, or =.

1 25 ◯ 25

2 22 ◯ 23

3 46 ◯ 45

4 26 ◯ 27

5 72 ◯ 71

6 76 ◯ 71

7 10 ◯ 11

8 32 ◯ 31

9 38 ◯ 39

10 45 ◯ 41

11 54 ◯ 51

12 87 ◯ 89

Army Ants

Read the article. Then answer the questions.

Army ants move in big groups. They march together to find food. Nothing stops them. Not even big holes.

Some army ants team up. They hook legs to make a chain. More ants hook on. The chain grows. The ant chain soon reaches across the hole. It's like a bridge. Other ants cross it.

At last the ants unhook and march on.

1 Army ants are special because they move
   O slowly.   O in water.   O in big groups.

2 What stops army ants from finding food?
   O big holes   O rain   O nothing

3 How do the ants team up?
   O They hook legs to make a chain.
   O They follow each other.
   O They stand on one another.

4 What can you tell about army ants from the picture?

_____

_____

_____

Mixed Math

How many tens and ones are in each number?
Write your answer on the lines. The first one is done for you.

53 = __5__ tens __3__ ones   70 = ____ tens ____ ones

68 = ____ tens ____ ones   25 = ____ tens ____ ones

49 = ____ tens ____ ones   31 = ____ tens ____ ones

Fast Practice
Add doubles.

$$6 + 6 = \square \qquad 9 + 9 = \square \qquad 7 + 7 = \square \qquad 8 + 8 = \square \qquad 5 + 5 = \square$$

Solve It!

A garden snake is 11 inches long. A milk snake is 4 inches shorter. Draw the snakes. How long is the milk snake?

Show your work.

A milk snake is _____ inches long.

Answer Key

Week 1

Punctuation Power

Each sentence is missing a punctuation mark.
Draw a line to match each punctuation mark to a sentence.

1. Let's go
2. I am a kid
3. Why doesn't the clock work
4. Do you have a hat
5. This game is fun
6. I play soccer
7. What's your name
8. The beach is great
9. My name is Paul

.
!
?
.
!
?
.
!
?

Shapes on a Snake

Write the number for each shape. Add or subtract.

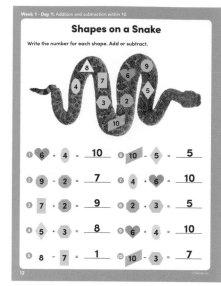

1. ♥ + ◆ = **10**
2. ⬡ − ◆ = **7**
3. ⬡ + ◆ = **9**
4. ◆ + ⬡ = **8**
5. ⬡ ◆ = **1**
6. ⬡ − ◆ = **5**
7. ◆ + ♥ = **10**
8. ◆ + ◆ = **5**
9. ♥ + ◆ = **10**
10. ◇ − ◆ = **7**

Capitalizing Names and First Words

Read each sentence.
Fill in the circle next to the word that needs a capital letter.

1. i like the goat named Gruff.
   ○ Goats
   ○ The
   ● I
2. I read the story with ron.
   ○ Read
   ○ Story
   ● Ron
3. Little gruff had a problem.
   ○ Had
   ● Gruff
   ○ Problem
4. troll was on the bridge.
   ○ On
   ○ Bridge
   ● Troll
5. His name was nosey.
   ○ Name
   ● Nosey
   ○ His

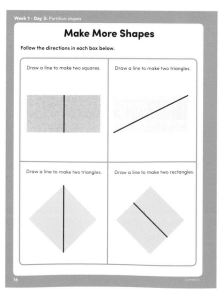

Tool Time

How many leaves long is each object? Write the answer on the line.

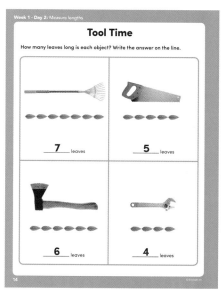

7 leaves

5 leaves

6 leaves

4 leaves

Hunt for Short a

Write the word for each picture. Use the Word Bank.
Then find and circle the words in the word search.

Word Bank

| apple | cat | ham | map | rat | van |

cat
apple
ham
rat
map
van

a c a t m
p c h a a
v a n p
l m h a m
e r a t p

Look at the pictures in each box. Say the names.
X the picture in each box that does not have a short-a sound.

Make More Shapes

Follow the directions in each box below.

Draw a line to make two squares.

Draw a line to make two triangles.

Draw a line to make two triangles.

Draw a line to make two rectangles.

Big the Pig

Read the story. Then answer each question.
Fill in the bubble next to the best answer.

My name is Ted. I live in Texas. I have a pig. My pig's name is Big. Big lives in a pen. He plays in the mud. He eats apples and corn. Big is a very big pig!

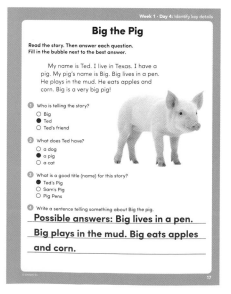

1. Who is telling the story?
   ○ Big
   ● Ted
   ○ Ted's friend
2. What does Ted have?
   ○ a dog
   ● a pig
   ○ a cat
3. What is a good title (name) for this story?
   ● Ted's Pig
   ○ Sam's Pig
   ○ Pig Pens
4. Write a sentence telling something about Big the pig.

Possible answers: Big lives in a pen. Big plays in the mud. Big eats apples and corn.

Solve the Riddle

Read the words and write the number. Solve the riddle using your answers.

two tens and ten ones	five tens and thirteen ones
30	**63**
F	I
four tens and sixteen ones	five tens and sixteen ones
56	**66**
S	M
two tens and fifteen ones	two tens and twenty ones
35	**40**
E	B
one ten and eighteen ones	seven tens and seventeen ones
28	**87**
R	A
eight tens and eleven ones	six tens and twelve ones
91	**72**
N	P

Write the letter that goes with each number.
What animal never tells the truth?

A M F I B I A N S
87 66 30 63 40 63 87 91 56

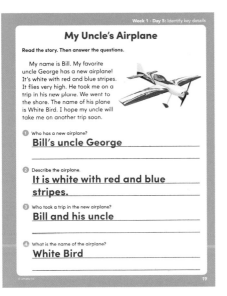

My Uncle's Airplane

Week 1 · Day 5: Identify key details

Read the story. Then answer the questions.

My name is Bill. My favorite uncle George has a new airplane! It's white with red and blue stripes. It flies very high. He took me on a trip in his new plane. We went to the shore. The name of his plane is White Bird. I hope my uncle will take me on another trip soon.

1. Who has a new airplane?
Bill's uncle George

2. Describe the airplane.
It is white with red and blue stripes.

3. Who took a trip in the new airplane?
Bill and his uncle

4. What is the name of the airplane?
White Bird

19

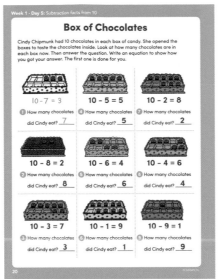

Box of Chocolates

Week 1 · Day 5: Subtraction facts from 10

Cindy Chipmunk had 10 chocolates in each box of candy. She opened the boxes to taste the chocolates inside. Look at how many chocolates are in each box now. Then answer the question. Write an equation to show how you got your answer. The first one is done for you.

$10 - 7 = 3$

$10 - 5 = 5$ | $10 - 2 = 8$
1. How many chocolates did Cindy eat? **7** | How many chocolates did Cindy eat? **5** | How many chocolates did Cindy eat? **2**

$10 - 8 = 2$ | $10 - 6 = 4$ | $10 - 4 = 6$
2. How many chocolates did Cindy eat? **8** | How many chocolates did Cindy eat? **6** | How many chocolates did Cindy eat? **4**

$10 - 3 = 7$ | $10 - 1 = 9$ | $10 - 9 = 1$
3. How many chocolates did Cindy eat? **3** | How many chocolates did Cindy eat? **1** | How many chocolates did Cindy eat? **9**

20

Week 2

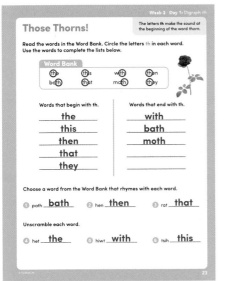

Those Thorns!

Week 2 · Day 1: Digraph th

The letters **th** make the sound at the beginning of the word *thorn*.

Read the words in the Word Bank. Circle the letters **th** in each word. Use the words to complete the lists below.

Word Bank
the · this · with · then · bath · that · moth · they

Words that begin with th.
the
this
then
that
they

Words that end with th.
with
bath
moth

Choose a word from the Word Bank that rhymes with each word.
1. path **bath**   2. hen **then**   3. rat **that**

Unscramble each word.
4. het **the**   5. hiwt **with**   6. tsih **this**

23

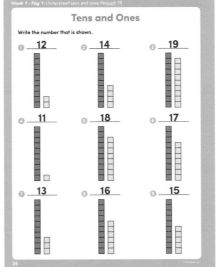

Tens and Ones

Week 2 · Day 1: Understand tens and ones through 19

Write the number that is shown.

1. **12**   2. **14**   3. **19**
4. **11**   5. **18**   6. **17**
7. **13**   8. **16**   9. **15**

24

Hunt for Short *e*

Week 2 · Day 2: Short-e vowel sound

Write the word for each picture. Use the Word Bank. Then find and circle the words in the word search.

Word Bank
bed · dress · egg · nest · ten · web

bed
nest
dress
ten
web
egg

Look at the picture. Fill in the circle next to the sentence that tells about the picture.
● This room is a mess!
○ His room is a map!

25

Crack the Code!

Week 2 · Day 2: Addition within 20

Solve these math problems. Use your answers to solve the riddle below.

$11 + 6$	$15 + 5$	$8 + 6$	$10 + 6$	$11 + 4$
17	**20**	**14**	**16**	**15**
R	H	S	O	Y

$10 + 2$	$11 + 2$	$9 + 2$	$12 + 6$
12	**13**	**11**	**18**
U	P	E	M

Now, put the letters in the correct spaces below.

What did the bunny say to the frog at the start of summer?

H O P P Y
20 16 13 13 15

S U M M E R
14 12 18 18 11 17

26

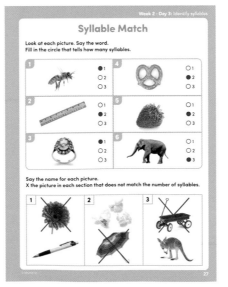

Syllable Match

Week 2 · Day 3: Identify syllables

Look at each picture. Say the word. Fill in the circle that tells how many syllables.

1. ●1 ○2 ○3   4. ○1 ●2 ○3
2. ○1 ●2 ○3   5. ○1 ●2 ○3
3. ●1 ○2 ○3   6. ○1 ○2 ●3

Say the name for each picture. X the picture in each section that does not match the number of syllables.

1   2   3

27

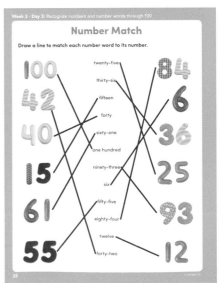

Number Match

Week 2 · Day 3: Recognize numbers and number words through 100

Draw a line to match each number word to its number.

100
42
40
15
61
55

twenty-five
thirty-six
fifteen
forty
sixty-one
one hundred
ninety-three
six
fifty-five
eighty-four
twelve
forty-two

84
6
36
25
93
12

28

131

Hunt for Short *i*

Write the word for each picture. Use the Word Bank.
Then find and circle the words in the word search.

Word Bank

fish	milk	pin	ship	six	zip

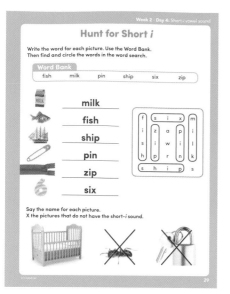

milk
fish
ship
pin
zip
six

f	s	i	x	m
i	z	a	p	i
s	i	w	w	l
h	r	i	r	k
s	h	i	p	s

Say the name for each picture.
X the pictures that do not have the short-*i* sound.

Greater Than or Less Than?

Compare the numbers. Use the number line.
Write > or < in each number sentence.

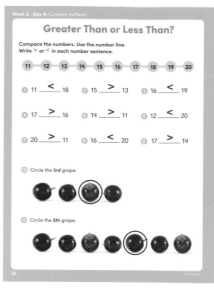

11 12 13 14 15 16 17 18 19 20

1. 11 < 18
2. 15 > 13
3. 16 < 19
4. 17 > 16
5. 14 > 11
6. 12 < 20
7. 20 > 11
8. 16 < 20
9. 17 > 14

10. Circle the **3rd** grape.

11. Circle the **5th** grape.

Life in the Ocean

Read about life in the ocean. Then answer the questions.

Dolphins live in the wide, open sea. They **roam** the ocean to catch fish. Dolphins do not swim too deep. They must come up to breathe.

Anglerfish live in the deep dark sea. They make their own light with a light pole. The light pole grows on top of their head! What happens when other fish swim toward the light? The anglerfish catches them!

Dolphins

Anglerfish

1. How are dolphins and anglerfish alike?
   - ● Both live in the sea.
   - ○ Both have a light pole.
   - ○ Both need to breathe air.

2. How are anglerfish and dolphins different?
   - ○ Anglerfish eat fish.
   - ● Anglerfish live in the deep sea.
   - ○ Dolphins can swim.

3. In the first paragraph, the word **roam** means
   - ○ part of a home.
   - ○ look for.
   - ● move from place to place.

Ready for Bed

Draw a line to match the clocks on the cat with the digital clocks.

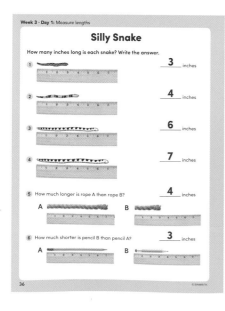

5:30 9:00 3:00 1:00 11:30 7:30 4:30 8:00

Week 3

Field Trip

Take a field trip to a farm! Say the name for each picture. Circle the word that matches each picture, then write it. Tell a story about the field trip.

bus (buses) — **buses**
(puppies) puppy — **puppies**
(chicks) chick — **chicks**
lamb (lambs) — **lambs**

Look at the picture. Fill in the missing letters. Use the Letter Bank. Read the sentence.

Letter Bank
s   es

The kitten **s** are sitting in their dish **e s** !

Silly Snake

How many inches long is each snake? Write the answer.

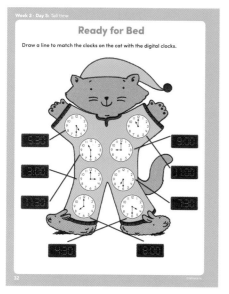

1. 3 inches
2. 4 inches
3. 6 inches
4. 7 inches

5. How much longer is rope A than rope B? 4 inches
   A
   B

6. How much shorter is pencil B than pencil A? 3 inches
   A
   B

Shiny Shells

The letters **sh** make the sound at the beginning of the word *shell*.

Read the words in the Word Bank. Circle the letters **sh** in each word.
Use the words to complete the lists below.

Word Bank

ship   she   fish   shape
wish   brush   shine   shoe

Words that begin with sh.
ship
she
shape
shine
shoe

Words that end with sh.
fish
wish
brush

Circle the word that is spelled correctly.

1. shipe (ship)
2. (shape) shap
3. (she) shee
4. (fish) fich
5. brosh (brush)
6. wich (wish)

I Can Count to 120!

This chart is missing some numbers. Fill in the missing numbers.

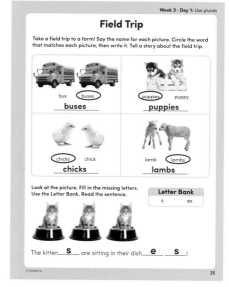

1	2	3	4	5	6	7	8	9	10
11	12	13	14	15	16	17	18	19	20
21	22	23	24	25	26	27	28	29	30
31	32	33	34	35	36	37	38	39	40
41	42	43	44	45	46	47	48	49	50
51	52	53	54	55	56	57	58	59	60
61	62	63	64	65	66	67	68	69	70
71	72	73	74	75	76	77	78	79	80
81	82	83	84	85	86	87	88	89	90
91	92	93	94	95	96	97	98	99	100
101	102	103	104	105	106	107	108	109	110
111	112	113	114	115	116	117	118	119	120

Hunt for Short o

Write the word for each picture. Use the Word Bank.
Then find and circle the words in the word search.

Word Bank

box	doll	fox	sock	stop	top

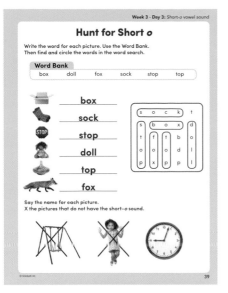

- box
- sock
- stop
- doll
- top
- fox

Say the name for each picture.
X the pictures that do not have the short-o sound.

39

Mixed Math

Draw lines to make matches.

1 ten 0 ones — 13
1 ten 1 one — 14
1 ten 2 ones — 11
1 ten 3 ones — 12
1 ten 4 ones — 10

1 ten 5 ones — 18
1 ten 6 ones — 15
1 ten 7 ones — 19
1 ten 8 ones — 16
1 ten 9 ones — 17

Fast Practice
Subtract.

$6 - 1 = $ **5** $5 - 2 = $ **3** $4 - 3 = $ **1**

$5 - 3 = $ **2** $4 - 2 = $ **2** $6 - 2 = $ **4**

Solve It!
Read each sentence. Draw and label the children from tallest to shortest.

Kim is shorter than Rob.   Max is taller than Rob.   Max is taller than Kim.

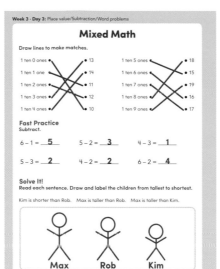

Max   Rob   Kim

40

Whose Is It?

A **noun** can show who owns something. This is done by adding an (') and s.

Joe is going on a trip. He needs to pack everything on his list.
Each object belongs to a different family member.

Study the picture to learn who owns each item.
Write it on the suitcase. The first one is done for you.

Kevin   Sam   Joe   Dad   Fred   Mom

skateboard   hat   bone
bowl   sunglasses   teddy bear

1 Kevin's skateboard   4 Dad's sunglasses
2 Sam's bowl   5 Fred's bone
3 Emma's teddy bear   6 Mom's hat

41

Use a Number Line

Find the sum. Use the number line to help you.

0 1 2 3 4 5 6 7 8 9 10 11 12 13 14 15 16 17 18 19 20

1 $8 + 8 = $ **16**   7 $7 + 6 = $ **13**

2 $11 + 4 = $ **15**   8 $3 + 15 = $ **18**

3 $8 + 6 = $ **14**   9 $7 + 5 = $ **12**

4 $4 + 12 = $ **16**   10 $12 + 3 = $ **15**

5 $11 + 7 = $ **18**   11 $5 + 5 = $ **10**

6 $6 + 5 = $ **11**   12 $4 + 15 = $ **19**

42

Fact or Fiction

Read the story. Then answer the questions.

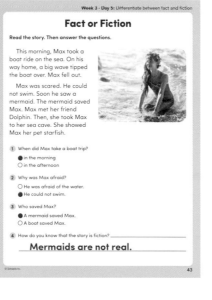

This morning, Max took a boat ride on the sea. On his way home, a big wave tipped the boat over. Max fell out.

Max was scared. He could not swim. Soon he saw a mermaid. The mermaid saved Max. Max met her friend Dolphin. Then, she took Max to her sea cave. She showed Max her pet starfish.

1 When did Max take a boat trip?
   ● in the morning
   ○ in the afternoon

2 Why was Max afraid?
   ○ He was afraid of the water.
   ● He could not swim.

3 Who saved Max?
   ● A mermaid saved Max.
   ○ A boat saved Max.

4 How do you know that the story is fiction? _____
   Mermaids are not real.

43

What's the Missing Sum?

Find the missing sum. Use the commutative property.

1 $3 + 5 = 8$ 6 $4 + 1 = 5$
   $5 + 3 = $ **8** $1 + 4 = $ **5**

2 $7 + 2 = 9$ 7 $1 + 2 = 3$
   $2 + 7 = $ **9** $2 + 1 = $ **3**

3 $5 + 2 = 7$ 8 $4 + 2 = 6$
   $2 + 5 = $ **7** $2 + 4 = $ **6**

4 $1 + 3 = 4$ 9 $2 + 3 = 5$
   $3 + 1 = $ **4** $3 + 2 = $ **5**

5 $4 + 5 = 9$ 10 $1 + 7 = 8$
   $5 + 4 = $ **9** $7 + 1 = $ **8**

44

Week 4

Hunt for Short u

Write the word for each picture. Use the Word Bank.
Then find and circle the words in the word search.

Word Bank

bug	bus	drum	rug	skunk	sun

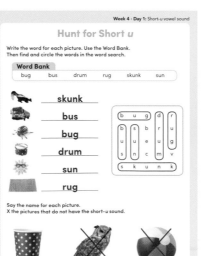

- skunk
- bus
- bug
- drum
- sun
- rug

Say the name for each picture.
X the pictures that do not have the short-u sound.

47

Kickboard Match Up

Add or subtract. Draw a line to match kickboards with the same answer.

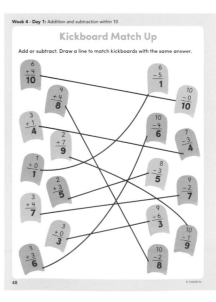

$\frac{6}{+4}$ **10** $\frac{6}{-5}$ **1**

$\frac{4}{+4}$ **8** $\frac{10}{-0}$ **10**

$\frac{3}{+1}$ **4** $\frac{10}{-4}$ **6**

$\frac{2}{+7}$ **9** $\frac{7}{-3}$ **4**

$\frac{0}{+1}$ **1** $\frac{8}{-3}$ **5**

$\frac{2}{+3}$ **5** $\frac{9}{-2}$ **7**

$\frac{3}{+4}$ **7** $\frac{9}{-0}$ **9**

$\frac{3}{+0}$ **3** $\frac{10}{-1}$ **9**

$\frac{3}{+3}$ **6** $\frac{10}{-2}$ **8**

48

133

Play Time

It's time to play! Say the name for each picture.
Circle the word, then write it. Use the words to tell a story.

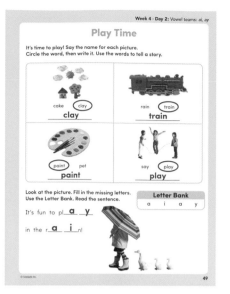

cake (clay)
clay

rain (train)
train

(paint) pet
paint

say (play)
play

Look at the picture. Fill in the missing letters.
Use the Letter Bank. Read the sentence.

Letter Bank
a i a y

It's fun to pl**a y**

in the r**a i**n!

49

Penguin Parade

Add or subtract.

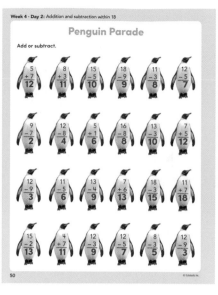

5 + 7 = **12**	8 + 3 = **11**	15 − 5 = **10**	18 − 9 = **9**	11 − 3 = **8**	12 − 5 = **7**
9 − 7 = **2**	8 − 4 = **4**	5 + 1 = **6**	16 − 8 = **8**	13 − 3 = **10**	7 + 5 = **12**
12 − 9 = **3**	11 − 5 = **6**	13 − 4 = **9**	7 + 6 = **13**	18 − 3 = **15**	11 + 7 = **18**
15 − 2 = **13**	4 + 7 = **11**	12 − 3 = **9**	12 − 5 = **7**	8 − 3 = **5**	12 − 9 = **3**

50

Multiple-Meaning Words

Complete each sentence with a word from the balloon that can be used in both blanks in each sentence. The first one is done for you.

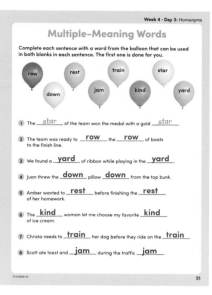

row   rest   train   star
down   jam   kind   yard

1. The **star** of the team won the medal with a gold **star**.
2. The team was ready to **row** the **row** of boats to the finish line.
3. We found a **yard** of ribbon while playing in the **yard**.
4. Juan threw the **down** pillow **down** from the top bunk.
5. Amber wanted to **rest** before finishing the **rest** of her homework.
6. The **kind** woman let me choose my favorite **kind** of ice cream.
7. Christa needs to **train** her dog before they ride on the **train**.
8. Scott ate toast and **jam** during the traffic **jam**.

51

Using a Number Line

Find the sum. Use the number line to help you.

0 1 2 3 4 5 6 7 8 9 10 11 12 13 14 15 16 17 18 19 20

1. 2 + 3 + 4 = **9**
2. 7 + 3 + 3 = **13**
3. 5 + 5 + 5 = **15**
4. 8 + 1 + 8 = **17**
5. 1 + 6 + 1 = **8**
6. 7 + 4 + 2 = **13**
7. 8 + 5 + 2 = **15**
8. 2 + 6 + 3 = **11**
9. 3 + 5 + 7 = **15**
10. 4 + 8 + 7 = **19**
11. 5 + 6 + 9 = **20**
12. 4 + 3 + 3 = **10**

52

Hunt for Long a and Long i

Write the word for each picture. Use the Word Bank.
Then find and circle the words in the word search.

Word Bank
bike   five   mice   rake   skate   whale

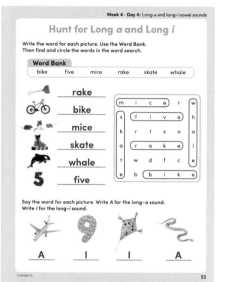

rake
bike
mice
skate
whale
five

m	i	c	e	r	w
s	f	i	v	e	h
k	r	t	s	o	a
a	r	a	k	e	l
t	w	d	f	c	e
e	b	i	k	e	b

Say the word for each picture. Write A for the long-a sound.
Write I for the long-i sound.

A   **I**   **I**   **A**

53

Mixed Math

How many tens are in each number? How many ones are there?
Write your answer on the lines. The first one is done for you.

26 = **2** tens 6 ones   54 = 5 tens **4** ones
47 = **4** tens 7 ones   82 = 8 tens **2** ones
39 = **3** tens 9 ones   75 = 7 tens **5** ones

Fast Practice
Subtract. Think about doubles.

10 − 5 = **5**   8 − 4 = **4**   6 − 3 = **3**
6 − **3** = 3   4 − **2** = 2   14 − **7** = 7

Solve It!
Libby has a nickel. Then she finds 2 pennies.
How much money does Libby have now?

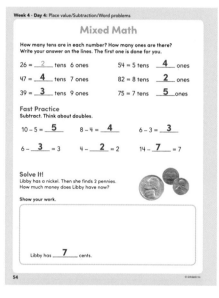

Show your work.

Libby has **7** cents.

54

The Biggest Spoon

**Read the paragraph.
Then answer the questions.**

What is the biggest spoon in the world? It is a group of bright stars called the Big Dipper. On a **clear** night, look up at the sky. The Big Dipper might be right side up. It might be upside down! People can use the Big Dipper to find their way when they get lost.

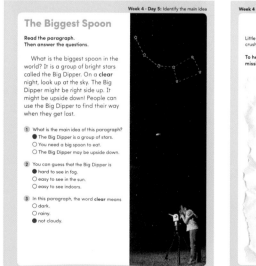

1. What is the main idea of this paragraph?
   ● The Big Dipper is a group of stars.
   ○ You need a big spoon to eat.
   ○ The Big Dipper may be upside down.

2. You can guess that the Big Dipper is
   ● hard to see in fog.
   ○ easy to see in the sun.
   ○ easy to see indoors.

3. In this paragraph, the word **clear** means
   ○ dark.
   ○ rainy.
   ● not cloudy.

55

Little Pig's Problem

Little Pig has a big problem! His homework got crushed in his book bag, and now he can't read it.

To help Little Pig fix his homework, find each missing number. Then write the number in the box.

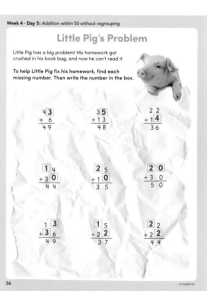

4 3 + 6 4 9	3 5 + 1 3 4 8	2 2 + 1 **4** 3 6
1 **4** + 3 0 4 4	2 5 + 1 0 3 5	2 **0** + 3 0 5 0
1 3 + 3 **6** 4 9	1 5 + 2 2 3 7	2 2 + 2 2 4 4

56

Week 5

Panel 1 (page 59)

What Happened?

Some **verbs** add *-ed* to tell about actions that happened in the past.

Read the first sentence in each pair.
Change the underlined verb to tell about the past.

1. Today, my dogs <u>push</u> open the back door.
   Yesterday, my dogs **pushed** open the back door.

2. Today, they <u>splash</u> in the rain puddles.
   Last night, they **splashed** in the rain puddles.

3. Now, they <u>roll</u> in the mud.
   Last week, they **rolled** in the mud.

4. Today, I <u>follow</u> my dogs' footprints.
   Last Sunday, I **followed** my dogs' footprints.

5. Now, I <u>wash</u> my dogs from head to toe.
   Earlier, I **washed** my dogs from head to toe.

Write a sentence using one of the verbs you wrote.

Sentences will vary.

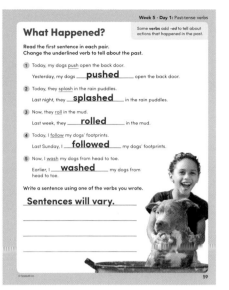

59

Panel 2 (page 60)

Tens and Ones

Write the number that is shown.

1. **38**
2. **23**
3. **45**
4. **64**
5. **57**
6. **43**
7. **56**

60

Panel 3 (page 61)

Hunt for Long *o* and Long *u*

Write the word for each picture. Use the Word Bank.
Then find and circle the words in the search.

Word Bank

bone	cone	cube	mule	nose	rose

- **cube**
- **bone**
- **mule**
- **cone**
- **nose**
- **rose**

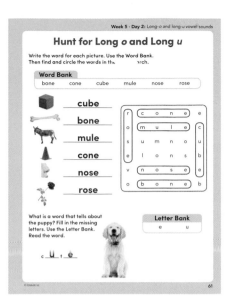

What is a word that tells about the puppy? Fill in the missing letters. Use the Letter Bank. Read the word.

Letter Bank

e	u

c _u_ t _e_

61

Panel 4 (page 62)

In Real Life . . .

Put on your thinking cap and circle each answer.

1. In real life, which one is the longest?

2. In real life, which one is the tallest?

62

Panel 5 (page 63)

Why Change?

The letters **ch** make the sound at the beginning of the word chain.

The letters **wh** make the sound at the beginning of the word wheel.

Read the words in the Word Bank.
Circle the letters **ch** and **wh** in each word.
Use the words to complete the lists below.

Word Bank

(chin) (chop) (whale) (when)
(inch) (which) (why) (what)

Words that start with **ch**.	Words that end with **ch**.	Words that start with **wh**.
chin	inch	whale
chop	which	when
		which
		why
		what

Write the word from the Word Bank that rhymes with each word below.

1. tail **whale**
2. mop **chop**
3. pinch **inch**
4. pitch **which**
5. pen **when**
6. win **chin**

63

Panel 6 (page 64)

Adding Numbers

Find the sum. Use the hundreds chart to help you.

1	2	3	4	5	6	7	8	9	10
11	12	13	14	15	16	17	18	19	20
21	22	23	24	25	26	27	28	29	30
31	32	33	34	35	36	37	38	39	40
41	42	43	44	45	46	47	48	49	50
51	52	53	54	55	56	57	58	59	60
61	62	63	64	65	66	67	68	69	70
71	72	73	74	75	76	77	78	79	80
81	82	83	84	85	86	87	88	89	90
91	92	93	94	95	96	97	98	99	100

1. 14 + 5 = **19**
2. 11 + 5 = **16**
3. 27 + 8 = **35**
4. 41 + 8 = **49**
5. 64 + 6 = **70**
6. 81 + 7 = **88**
7. 15 + 6 = **21**
8. 22 + 6 = **28**
9. 35 + 7 = **42**
10. 56 + 9 = **65**
11. 73 + 9 = **82**
12. 93 + 6 = **99**

64

Panel 7 (page 65)

What an End!

Add –ing and –ed to each base word in the chart. One row is done for you.

Base Word	–ing	–ed
1. show	showing	showed
2. lick	licking	licked
3. plant	planting	planted
4. brush	brushing	brushed
5. walk	walking	walked
6. play	playing	played

Complete each sentence. Use a word from the chart above.
The first one is done for you.

Possible answers shown.

7. Yesterday, I _planted_ two new trees.
8. Earlier, I **showed** Martha my bike.
9. Today, I am **playing** with Jake and Will.
10. Earlier this morning, I **walked** to Grandma's.

65

Panel 8 (page 66)

See Our Seashells

Use the graph to answer the questions.

Seashells We Found

Ming	Danny	Eva	Jack

1. How many children found shells? **4**
2. How many shells did the children find in all? **16**
3. Who found the fewest shells? **Eva**
4. Two children found 4 shells each. Write their names.
   Ming and **Jack**
5. Who found the most shells? **Danny**

66

Panel 9 (page 67)

Twins

Holly and Polly are twins. They are in the first grade. They look alike, but they are very different. Holly likes to play softball and soccer. She likes to wear her hair braided when she goes out to play. She wears sporty clothes. Recess is her favorite part of school. Polly likes to read books and paint pictures. Every day she wears a ribbon in her hair to match her dress. Her favorite thing about school is going to the library. She wants to be a teacher some day.

Look at the pictures of Holly and Polly. They look alike but there are differences. Can you find them? Circle the things that are different.

I like to play softball. Holly
I like to read and paint. Polly

Your child should circle: both girls' hair, clothes, and shoes; Holly's baseball and bat; Molly's paintbrush and book.

Underline the sentence that tells what is the same about Holly and Polly.

They play sports.   They love to paint.   <u>They are in the first grade.</u>

67

Complete the Shape

Draw the other half of each shape. Example:

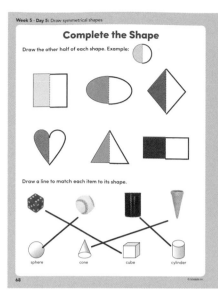

Draw a line to match each item to its shape.

sphere   cone   cube   cylinder

68   © Scholastic Inc.

Week 6

In the Garden

What's growing in this garden? Say the name for each picture.
Circle the word, then write it. Use the words to tell a story.

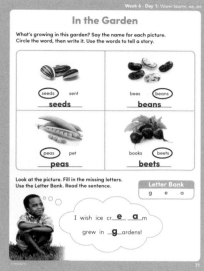

(seeds) sent	bees (beans)
seeds	**beans**
(peas) pet	books (beets)
peas	**beets**

Look at the picture. Fill in the missing letters.
Use the Letter Bank. Read the sentence.

Letter Bank
g e a

I wish ice cr__e__ __a__m
grew in __g__ardens!

71

How Long Is It?

How many erasers long is each item? Write the answer.

1. __5__ erasers
2. __2__ erasers
3. __3__ erasers
4. __4__ erasers

5. Circle the longest object.

6. Circle the shortest object.

72   © Scholastic Inc.

Four Seasons on a Farm

What happens throughout the year on a farm?
Look at each picture. Circle the word for each picture, then write it.
Use the words to tell a story about a farm.

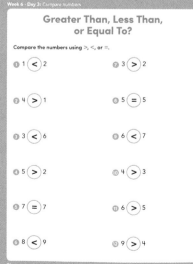

(hoe) hop	boat (grow)
hoe	**grow**
(mow) more	saw (snow)
mow	**snow**

Look at the picture fill in the missing letters.
Use the Letter Bank. Read the sentence.

Letter Bank
o a

A baby horse is a f__o__ __a__l.

73

What Time Is It?

Look at the clocks below. Write the time each clock shows.

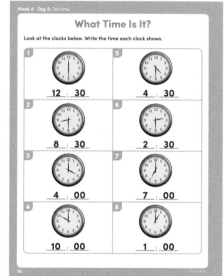

1. __12__ : __30__
2. __8__ : __30__
3. __4__ : __00__
4. __10__ : __00__
5. __4__ : __30__
6. __2__ : __30__
7. __7__ : __00__
8. __1__ : __00__

74

It's Raining

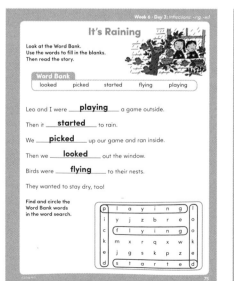

Look at the Word Bank.
Use the words to fill in the blanks.
Then read the story.

Word Bank
looked   picked   started   flying   playing

Leo and I were __playing__ a game outside.

Then it __started__ to rain.

We __picked__ up our game and ran inside.

Then we __looked__ out the window.

Birds were __flying__ to their nests.

They wanted to stay dry, too!

Find and circle the
Word Bank words
in the word search.

p	l	a	y	i	n	g	l
i	y	j	z	b	r	e	o
k	f	l	y	i	n	g	o
k	m	x	r	q	x	w	k
e	j	g	s	k	p	z	e
d	s	t	a	r	t	e	d

75

Greater Than, Less Than, or Equal To?

Compare the numbers using >, <, or =.

1. 1 < 2
2. 4 > 1
3. 3 < 6
4. 5 > 2
5. 7 = 7
6. 8 < 9
7. 3 > 2
8. 5 = 5
9. 6 < 7
10. 4 > 3
11. 6 > 5
12. 9 > 4

76   © Scholastic Inc.

Positional Words

Draw lines to connect each sentence to its picture.

Word Bank
on off over under before after up down around into

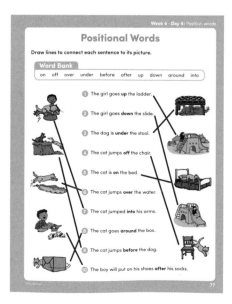

1. The girl goes **up** the ladder.
2. The girl goes **down** the slide.
3. The dog is **under** the stool.
4. The cat jumps **off** the chair.
5. The cat is **on** the bed.
6. The cat jumps **over** the water.
7. The cat jumped **into** his arms.
8. The cat goes **around** the box.
9. The cat jumps **before** the dog.
10. The boy will put on his shoes **after** his socks.

77

What's at the Store?

It's time to add up items at the toy store. Read each problem.
Then write an equation to answer the question.

1 7 toy kittens
5 toy puppies

7 + 5 = 12

How many toy animals are in the store? **12**

4 9 card games
6 board games

9 + 6 = 15

How many games are in the store? **15**

2 7 ring floats
6 flat floats

7 + 6 = 13

How many floats are in the store? **13**

5 6 fire trucks
8 dump trucks

6 + 8 = 14

How many toy trucks are in the store? **14**

3 9 talking books
8 pop-up books

9 + 8 = 17

How many books are in the store? **17**

6 4 footballs
7 baseballs

4 + 7 = 11

How many balls are in the store? **11**

A Dolphin Boat

Read the article. Then answer the questions.

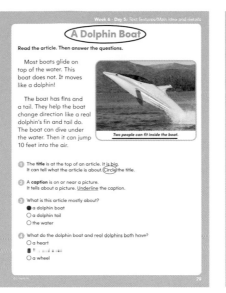

Most boats glide on top of the water. This boat does not. It moves like a dolphin!

The boat has fins and a tail. They help the boat change direction like a real dolphin's fin and tail do. The boat can dive under the water. Then it can jump 10 feet into the air.

Two people can fit inside the boat.

1 The **title** is at the top of an article. It is big.
It can tell what the article is about. Circle the title.

2 A **caption** is on or near a picture.
It tells about a picture. Underline the caption.

3 What is this article mostly about?
● a dolphin boat
○ a dolphin tail
○ the water

4 What do the dolphin boat and real dolphins both have?
○ a heart
● a fin and a tail
○ a wheel

Missing Sums

Find the missing number in the equation. Use the commutative property.

1 6 + 8 = 14
8 + 6 = **14**

2 9 + 2 = 11
2 + 9 = 11

3 4 + 3 = 7
3 + **4** = 7

7 9 + 7 = 16
7 + 9 = **16**

4 5 + 4 = 9
4 + 5 = **9**

8 7 + 5 = 12
5 + 7 = 12

5 9 + 8 = 17
8 + 9 = 17

9 1 + 9 = 10
9 + **1** = 10

6 9 + 5 = 14
5 + **9** = 14

10 10 + 6 = 16
6 + 10 = **16**

Week 7

A Tight Squeeze

The long-vowel sounds can be spelled with the following letters:

long a:	long e:	long i:	long o:
a_e, ay, ai	ee, e_e	i_e	o_e

Read the words in the Word Bank. Underline the letters that make the long-vowel sound in each word. Use the words to complete the lists below.

Word Bank

cake   nail   tray   seed
nine   nose   kite   here

Words with long-a sound	Words with long-e sound	Words with long-i sound	Words with long-o sound
cake	seed	nine	nose
nail	here	kite	
tray			

Write the word from the Word Bank that belongs with each group below.

1 nose **4** tray
2 seed **5** cake
3 nine **6** nail

Race Through the Facts

Add or subtract.
The race car that ends with the highest number wins the race!

The red car wins the race.

Commas in a Series

Some sentences include a list. A **comma** (,) is used to separate each item in the list.
For example: *Mrs. Jones asked the class to work on pages two, three, and four.*

Fill in the blanks to make a list in each sentence.
Watch for commas!

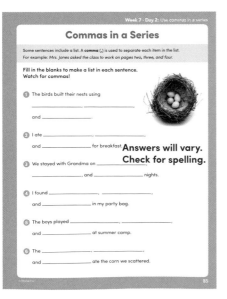

1 The birds built their nests using
_____, _____,
and _____.

2 I ate _____, _____,
and _____ for breakfast.

3 We stayed with Grandma on _____,
_____, and _____ nights.

4 I found _____, _____,
and _____ in my party bag.

5 The boys played _____, _____,
and _____ at summer camp.

6 The _____, _____,
and _____ ate the corn we scattered.

Answers will vary. Check for spelling.

Using a Number Line

Find the difference. Use the number line to help you.

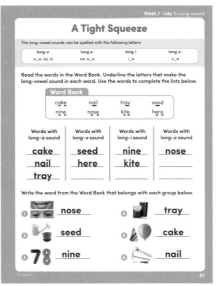

1 7 – 4 = **3**   **7** 8 – 3 = **5**

2 9 – 2 = **7**   **8** 6 – 4 = **2**

3 12 – 4 = **8**   **9** 14 – 5 = **9**

4 10 – 3 = **7**   **10** 9 – 7 = **2**

5 18 – 6 = **12** **11** 15 – 9 = **6**

6 11 – 7 = **4**   **12** 19 – 8 = **11**

Describing Words

Read each sentence. Trace the word. Next to each picture, write the number of the sentence that describes it. Read each sentence again. The first one is done for you.

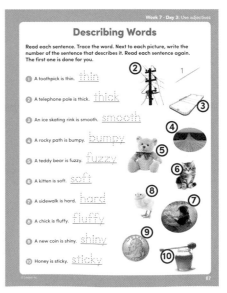

1 A toothpick is thin. thin

2 A telephone pole is thick. thick

3 An ice skating rink is smooth. smooth

4 A rocky path is bumpy. bumpy

5 A teddy bear is fuzzy. fuzzy

6 A kitten is soft. soft

7 A sidewalk is hard. hard

8 A chick is fluffy. fluffy

9 A new coin is shiny. shiny

10 Honey is sticky. sticky

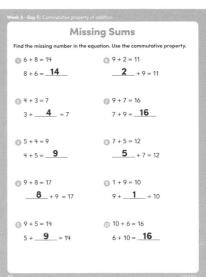

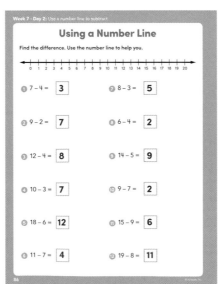

Describing Words

Write the best word to complete each sentence.

Word Bank
thin   fuzzy
soft   hard
fluffy

1. Cotton candy is **fluffy**
2. Before it is cooked, a potato is **hard**
3. A peach's skin is **fuzzy**
4. A needle is **thin**
5. Mashed potatoes are **soft**

Look at the words in the Word Bank.
Find and circle each word in the word search.

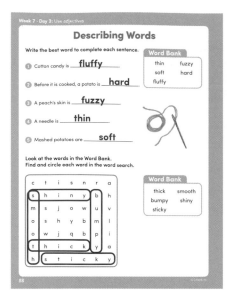

Word Bank
thick   smooth
bumpy   shiny
sticky

c	t	i	s	n	r	a
s	h	i	n	y	b	h
m	s	j	o	w	u	v
o	s	h	y	b	m	l
o	w	j	q	b	p	l
t	h	i	c	k	y	a
h	s	t	i	c	k	y

88

Check it Out!

The letters **ck** make the sound at the end of the word pick.

Read the words in the Word Bank. Circle the letters ck in each word. Use the words to complete the lists below.

Word Bank
duck   pack   stick   back
neck   rock   clock   quick

Words with short-*a* sound	Words with short-*e* sound	Words with short-*o* sound
pack	neck	rock
back		clock

Words with short-*i* sound	Words with short-*u* sound
stick	duck
quick	

Write the word from the Word Bank that best matches each picture.

1. **duck**
2. **rock**
3. **stick**
4. **clock**

89

Break the Code

Subtract.

6 − 2 = **4**	13 − 7 = **6**	17 − 7 = **10**	18 − 9 = **9**	15 − 8 = **7**
11 − 9 = **2**	9 − 4 = **5**	14 − 6 = **8**	11 − 8 = **3**	7 − 6 = **1**

Use the answers above to solve each problem.

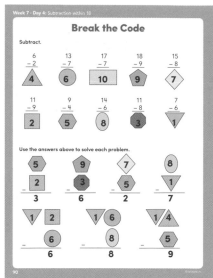

90

Going to Granny's

Read the story. Then answer the questions.

Kelly is going to spend the night with her grandmother. She will need to take her pajamas, a T-shirt, and some shorts. Into the suitcase go her toothbrush, toothpaste, and hairbrush. Granny told her to bring a swimsuit in case it was warm enough to swim. Mom said to pack her favorite pillow and storybook. Dad said, "Don't forget to take Granny's sunglasses that she left here last week." Now Kelly is ready to go!

1. Circle the things that Kelly packed in her suitcase.

2. A **compound word** is a word that is made up of two smaller words. For example, *cow* + *boy* = *cowboy*. Find and circle eight compound words in the story.

91

A Nutty Bunch

Add or subtract. Circle the nut if the answer matches the squirrel.

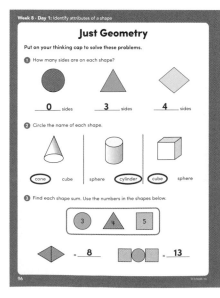

15 − 3 = 12   11 + 2 = 13
6 + 7 = 13   17 − 4 = 13
13

13 + 4 = 17   9 + 6 = 15
18 − 3 = 15   15 + 2 = 17
17

9 + 3 = 12   15 − 4 = 11
8 + 3 = 11   18 − 7 = 11
11

92

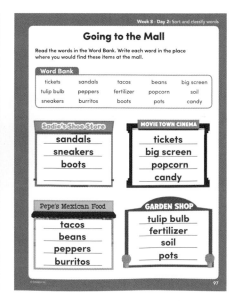

More Describing Words

How would you describe a lollipop or a baby chick? Complete the chart below with describing words for each. Choose words from the Word Bank.

Word Bank
thin   thick   smooth   bumpy   fuzzy
soft   hard   fluffy   shiny   sticky

Possible answers shown.

Lollipop	Chick
thin	fuzzy
hard	soft
sticky	fluffy
shiny	

1. Name something that is thin. **Answers will vary.**
2. Name something that is thick. _____
3. Name something that is bumpy. _____

95

Just Geometry

Put on your thinking cap to solve these problems.

1. How many sides are on each shape?

0 sides   **3** sides   **4** sides

2. Circle the name of each shape.

cone   cube   sphere   cylinder   cube   sphere

3. Find each shape sum. Use the numbers in the shapes below.

3   4   5

◇ = **8**   ▭◯▭ = **13**

96

Going to the Mall

Read the words in the Word Bank. Write each word in the place where you would find these items at the mall.

Word Bank
tickets   sandals   tacos   beans   big screen
tulip bulb   peppers   fertilizer   popcorn   soil
sneakers   burritos   boots   pots   candy

Sadie's Shoe Store
sandals
sneakers
boots

MOVIE TOWN CINEMA
tickets
big screen
popcorn
candy

Pepe's Mexican Food
tacos
beans
peppers
burritos

GARDEN SHOP
tulip bulb
fertilizer
soil
pots

97

Opposites Attract

Add or subtract. Draw a line to connect the magnets with the same answer. Read the words in each connecting set of magnets.

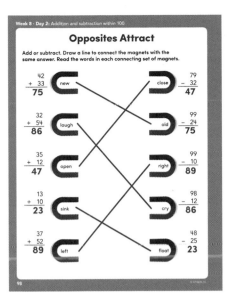

42 + 33 = **75** (new)	79 − 32 = **47** (close)
32 + 54 = **86** (laugh)	99 − 24 = **75** (old)
35 + 12 = **47** (open)	99 − 10 = **89** (right)
13 + 10 = **23** (sink)	98 − 12 = **86** (cry)
37 + 52 = **89** (left)	48 − 25 = **23** (float)

98

Same But Different

Circle the word that is almost the same as the first word.

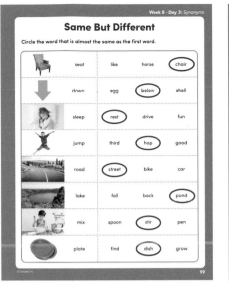

	seat	like	horse	(chair)
	down	egg	(below)	shell
	sleep	(rest)	drive	fun
	jump	third	(hop)	good
	road	(street)	bike	car
	lake	fall	back	(pond)
	mix	spoon	(stir)	pen
	plate	find	(dish)	grow

99

Multiples of 10

Find the difference. Use the hundreds chart to help you.

1	2	3	4	5	6	7	8	9	10
11	12	13	14	15	16	17	18	19	20
21	22	23	24	25	26	27	28	29	30
31	32	33	34	35	36	37	38	39	40
41	42	43	44	45	46	47	48	49	50
51	52	53	54	55	56	57	58	59	60
61	62	63	64	65	66	67	68	69	70
71	72	73	74	75	76	77	78	79	80
81	82	83	84	85	86	87	88	89	90
91	92	93	94	95	96	97	98	99	100

1. 50 − 10 = **40**
2. 70 − 10 = **60**
3. 80 − 30 = **50**
4. 70 − 60 = **10**
5. 80 − 60 = **20**
6. 60 − 10 = **50**
7. 20 − 10 = **10**
8. 50 − 20 = **30**
9. 90 − 20 = **70**
10. 40 − 30 = **10**
11. 70 − 40 = **30**
12. 90 − 30 = **60**

100

Moles, Voles, or Both?

Read. Then answer the questions.

Moles and Voles

Moles and voles are both found in North America. They are alike in many ways. They are also different. Both moles and voles are small animals. Both cause problems for gardeners. Moles and voles both dig a lot. This hurts gardens. Read below how moles and voles are different.

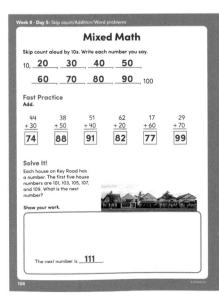

Only Moles
eat insects
have big paws
have long noses

Only Voles
eat plants
have small paws
have short noses

1. What can both animals hurt?
   gardens

2. Which animal eats plants?
   voles

3. Which animal has big paws?
   moles

101

Making Shapes

Some shapes are shown below. They have extra shapes next to them. Make a new shape by tracing the extra shapes. Then color in the shapes.

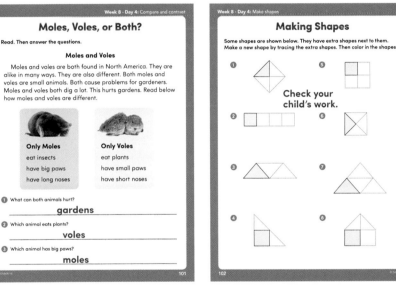

Check your child's work.

102

Trucks

Read about trucks. Then follow the directions below.

Trucks do important work. Dump trucks carry away sand and rocks. Cement trucks have a barrel that turns round and round. They deliver cement to workers who are making sidewalks. Fire trucks carry water hoses and firefighters. Gasoline is delivered in large tank trucks. Flat bed trucks carry wood to people who are building houses.

1. What is the main idea of the paragraph? Write it in the circle below.
2. Draw a line from the main idea to the trucks described in the paragraph.

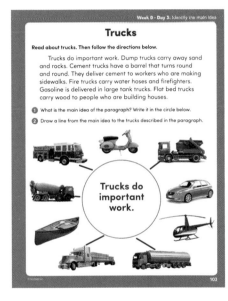

Trucks do important work.

103

Mixed Math

Skip count aloud by 10s. Write each number you say.

10, **20**, **30**, **40**, **50**, **60**, **70**, **80**, **90**, 100

Fast Practice
Add.

44 + 30	38 + 50	51 + 40	62 + 20	17 + 60	29 + 70
74	**88**	**91**	**82**	**77**	**99**

Solve It!
Each house on Key Road has a number. The first five house numbers are 101, 103, 105, 107, and 109. What is the next number?

Show your work.

The next number is **111**

104

Week 9

Find the Missing Letter

Consonants
Look at each picture. Write the missing letter to complete the word.

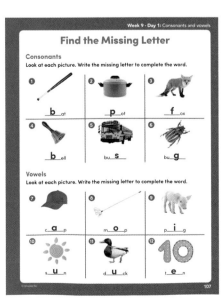

1. **b** at
2. **p** ot
3. **f** ox
4. **b** ell
5. bu **s**
6. bu **g**

Vowels
Look at each picture. Write the missing letter to complete the word.

7. c **a** p
8. m **o** p
9. p **i** g
10. s **u** n
11. d **u** ck
12. t **e** n

107

139

Add Multiples of 10

What number is 10 more? Use the hundreds chart to help you.

1. 72 + 10 = **82**
2. 28 + 10 = **38**
3. 54 + 10 = **64**
4. 32 + 10 = **42**

What is the sum? Use the hundreds chart to help you.

5. 26 + 50 = **76**
6. 38 + 30 = **68**
7. 17 + 60 = **77**
8. 42 + 40 = **82**

108

A Happy Camper

Complete each sentence below.

1. Every sentence begins with a **capital letter**
2. A statement ends with a **period**
3. A question ends with a **question mark**

Read Dalton's letter. It looks like he was in a hurry when he wrote it. Help him find ten mistakes. Circle them.

Dear Mom and Dad,

Camp is so cool. Today we went swimming. Do you know what I like best about camp? Fishing is my favorite thing to do. Did you feed my hamster? I really miss you.

Love,
Dalton

Choose two questions and two statements from Dalton's letter. Rewrite each correctly. **Choices will vary.**

4. **Do you know what I like best about camp?**
5. **Did you feed my hamster?**
6. **Today we went swimming.**
7. **I really miss you.**

109

Tick-Tock Clocks

Draw hands to show each time.

2:00   6:00

11:00   10:30

5:30   9:00

110

Going Swimming

Read the story.

Tomorrow I will go swimming. I will put on my swimsuit. I will jump in the water to get wet. Then I will dive off the diving board. Grandma will fix lunch for me. Mom will swim with me after lunch.

Read the sentences below.
Rewrite them in the correct order.

Mom will swim with me after lunch.
I will put on my swimsuit.
Grandma will fix lunch for me.
I will jump in the water.

1. **I will put on my swimsuit.**
2. **I will jump in the water.**
3. **Grandma will fix lunch for me.**
4. **Mom will swim with me after lunch.**

111

Ocean Math

Circle the two numbers that make 10. Then add. The first one is done for you. Solve the riddle using your answers.

⑤+⑤+ 10 = **20**

5 +③+⑦ **15** (I)

③+⑦+ 4 = **14** (W)

3 +⑥+④ **13** (S)

⑤+ 1 +⑤ **11** (R)

②+ 7 +⑧ **17** (E)

⑥+④+ 9 = **19** (V)

⑥+ 2 +④ **12** (N)

⑧+② 10 = **20** (A)

⑤+ 8 +⑤ **18** (T)

Write the letter that goes with each number.
What does the ocean do when it sees the beach?

I T   W A V E   S
15 18   14 20 19 17 13

112

Family Word Sort

Sort the words from the Word Bank. Then write them in the correct boxes.

Word Bank

mother father sister brother daughter
son baby grandma grandpa

Family
Adults Children

Adults
mother
father
grandma
grandpa

Children
sister
brother
son
daughter
baby

How else might you sort the words?
Possible answer: male/female

113

Animal Chart

Count each kind of animal. Show how many in the graph. Color one box for each animal you count.

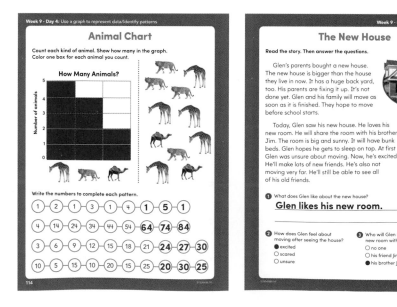

How Many Animals?

Number of animals (0–5)

Write the numbers to complete each pattern.

1 – 2 – 3 – 1 – 2 – 3 – 4 – 1 – **1** – **5** – **1**

4 – 14 – 24 – 34 – 44 – 54 – **64** – **74** – **84**

3 – 6 – 9 – 12 – 15 – 18 – 21 – **24** – **27** – **30**

10 – 5 – 20 – 15 – 20 – 15 – **20** – **30** – **25**

114

The New House

Read the story. Then answer the questions.

Glen's parents bought a new house. The new house is bigger than the house they live in now. It has a huge back yard, too. His parents are fixing it up. It's not done yet. Glen and his family will move as soon as it is finished. They hope to move before school starts.

Today, Glen saw his new house. He loves his new room. He will share the room with his brother Jim. The room is big and sunny. It will have bunk beds. Glen hopes he gets to sleep on top. At first Glen was unsure about moving. Now, he's excited. He'll make lots of new friends. He's also not moving very far. He'll still be able to see all of his old friends.

1. What does Glen like about the new house?
Glen likes his new room.

2. How does Glen feel about moving after seeing the house?
● excited
○ scared
○ unsure

3. Who will Glen share his new room with?
○ no one
○ his friend Jim
● his brother Jim

115

Mixed Math

Count back aloud by 10s. Write each number you say.

100, **90**, **80**, **70**, **60**, **50**, **40**, **30**, **20**, 10, 0

Fast Practice
Subtract.

85 − 60 = **25**
92 − 70 = **22**
51 − 40 = **11**
64 − 30 = **34**
78 − 50 = **28**
39 − 20 = **19**

Solve It!
The art teacher gets 32 new paintbrushes and 45 new markers. How many new art items is this in all?

Show your work.

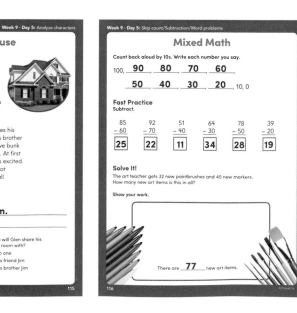

There are **77** new art items.

116

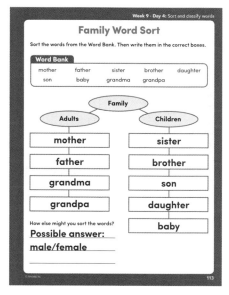

140

Week 10

Fill-In Story

Look at the pictures. Fill in the missing letters.
Use the Letter Bank. Then read the story.

Letter Bank
p d g f c

"Moo, moo," says the **c**ow.

"Baa, baa," says the shee**p**.

"Oink, oink," says the pi**g**.

"Quack, quack," says the **d**uck.

What a noisy **f**arm!

Say the name for each picture.
Fill in the missing letter. Use the Letter Bank.

Letter Bank
n c h

he**n**   **h**orse   **c**at

119

Shaping Up

Draw the shape shown in each box. Then color each shape.

Answers will vary.

Make your own.

120

Two-Way Words

Use the Letter Banks and pictures to complete each activity.

❶ Fill in the missing letters to make two words.

Letter Bank
f m s t

s i x / s u n / d r u m / j a **m**

f a n / d o g / g o a t / t e n t

❷ Fill in the missing letters. Read the word.

Letter Bank
d s

s**p**i**d**er

❸ Read each word below. Change one letter
to make a new word. Read the new word.

Letter Bank
r t

fun → **r**un   cap → ca**t**

121

Mixed Math

Write the number that is 10 less.

13 **3**   74 **64**   98 **88**

61 **51**   85 **75**   72 **62**

Fast Practice
Draw hands to show each time.

2:00	6:00	11:00

Solve It!
A zoo has 14 monkeys
and 11 parrots. Each gets
1 apple a day. How many
apples do all the animals
eat in 2 days?

Show your work.

They eat **50** apples in all.

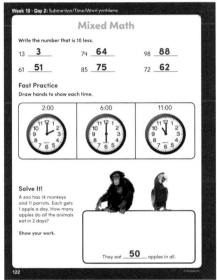

122

A Trip to the Movies

Use the price list to answer the questions.

Prices	
Child's Ticket	$8
Large Popcorn	$5
Small Popcorn	$4
Large Soda	$3
Small Soda	$2

Renee has $20. She goes to the movies.

❶ How much money does Renee have after she buys a ticket? **$12**

❷ Her dad told her to bring home $5. But Renee wants popcorn and soda.
What can she order? **small popcorn + large soda or large popcorn + small soda**

❸ How much would it cost for 4 children to buy movie tickets? **$32**

123

Corners and Sides

How many corners are in each shape?

❶ **4** corners   ❷ **4** corners   ❸ **6** corners

❹ **3** corners   ❺ **4** corners   ❻ **5** corners

How many sides are in each shape?

❼ square **4**
❽ triangle **3**
❾ rectangle **4**
❿ pentagon **5**

Draw three different shapes, each
with four corners and four sides.

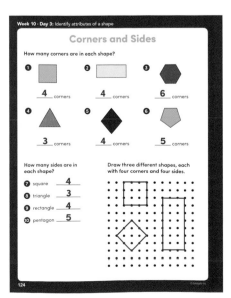

124

Mixed-Up Margie

Once upon a time there was a
mixed-up queen named Margie.
She got things mixed up. She wore her
crown on her arm. She wore a shoe on
her head. She painted every fingernail
a different color. Then she painted her
nose red! She used a fork to hold her
hair in place. She wore a purple belt
around her knees. The king didn't mind.
He alway wore his clothes backward!

*A character is a person or animal in
a story. To help readers understand
a character better, a story often gives
details about the character.*

Use the story and your crayons to help
you follow these instructions:

❶ Draw Margie a crown.   **Check your**
❷ Draw her shoe.   **child's work.**
❸ Paint her fingernails and nose.
❹ Draw what goes in her hair.
❺ Draw her belt.

Fill in the bubble next to the correct answer.

❻ What makes you think Margie is mixed up?
● the way she dresses
○ the way she talks

❼ What makes you think the king is mixed up, too?
○ He talks backward.
● He wears his clothes backward.

125

Compare Numbers

Compare the numbers. Use >, <, or =.

❶ 25 **=** 25   ❼ 10 **<** 11

❷ 22 **<** 23   ❽ 32 **>** 31

❸ 46 **>** 45   ❾ 38 **<** 39

❹ 26 **<** 27   ❿ 45 **>** 41

❺ 72 **>** 71   ⓫ 54 **>** 51

❻ 76 **>** 71   ⓬ 87 **<** 89

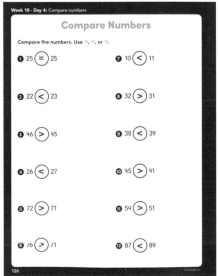

126

Army Ants

Read the article. Then answer the questions.

Army ants move in big groups. They march together to find food. Nothing stops them. Not even big holes.

Some army ants team up. They hook legs to make a chain. More ants hook on. The chain grows. The ant chain soon reaches across the hole. It's like a bridge. Other ants cross it.

At last the ants unhook and march on.

1 Army ants are special because they move
○ slowly.   ○ in water.   ● in big groups.

2 What stops army ants from finding food?
○ big holes   ○ rain   ● nothing

3 How do the ants team up?
● They hook legs to make a chain.
○ They follow each other.
○ They stand on one another.

4 What can you tell about army ants from the picture?

Answers will vary.

127

Mixed Math

How many tens and ones are in each number?
Write your answer on the lines. The first one is done for you.

53 = __5__ tens __3__ ones   70 = __7__ tens __0__ ones

68 = __6__ tens __8__ ones   25 = __2__ tens __5__ ones

49 = __4__ tens __9__ ones   31 = __3__ tens __1__ ones

Fast Practice
Add doubles.

$$\begin{array}{ccccc} 6 & 9 & 7 & 8 & 5 \\ +6 & +9 & +7 & +8 & +5 \\ \hline \boxed{12} & \boxed{18} & \boxed{14} & \boxed{16} & \boxed{10} \end{array}$$

Solve It!
A garden snake is 11 inches long. A milk snake is 4 inches shorter. Draw the snakes. How long is the milk snake?

Show your work.

A milk snake is __7__ inches long.

128

FOR OUTSTANDING ACHIEVEMENT

CONGRATULATIONS!

This certificate is awarded to

I'm proud of you!